# GOD IS JUST LIKE JESUS

**VOLUME 1**

## Jesus' Goodness during Our Failure and Sin

ISLU Publishing

CHRIS SARRIS

God Is Just Like Jesus - Volume 1 - Jesus' Goodness during Our Failure and Sin



Cover design by Rob Squire

ISLU Publishing
PO Box 135,
Niwot, CO 80544

ISBN: 978-1-7361547-0-0

To my brother Keith.
*In many ways I wrote this book for you. Now you know Him face to face.*

# TABLE OF CONTENTS

# ACKNOWLEDGMENTS

This book would not be here without the encouragement of so many people who have found worth in this material and kept me going!

First, my thanks go to my wife, Kirsty, for her emotional support, for her passion for Jesus, and for working so hard with me on this book. I wanted to add her name as an author on this book, but she wouldn't let me! Thanks to my two boys, Luke and Isaac, who always remind me of what's most important in life. My prayer has always been that I may be able to help you see that the good character of God is an "ark" of protection for you to nourish yourselves and rest in while living in this crazy world. I love you deeply!

Thanks to my mom who has always believed in me and loved me unconditionally. Thanks, Mom, for all your prayers behind the scenes to help bring this book to fruition.

To my brother Neil, I'm grateful for you. You, Keith, and I made it through a crazy childhood together. You are a great brother to me.

Special thanks also to the Mojo's Men Group. This book is here in part because you guys found value in it week after week! Thanks to Art Enns, Derek Reiger, Sean Von Roenn, Chuck Goertzen, Brad Prill, Brian Krueger, Andy Carter, David Kennedy, and Ted Lyke.

So many people have had input into this book with small group discussions, Zoom discussions, technical help, and ideas. A sincere voice of appreciation for Adrian Boykin, Mark Ludy, James Higgs, Andy Greenidge, Kim McConnell, Cameron Rake, Shawn Kroeger, Jacques Hueber, Tom Jordan, Joanne Irwin, Joy Goertzen, Jonah Peterson, Terry Mayes, Gretchen Lee, Mark Enns, Tracey and Greg Whipkey, John and Susan Ringoen, Caleb Chamberlain, our Calvary Erie lifegroup, our Flatirons small group, and so many other people. You know who you are, and I am grateful.

Thanks to Rob Squire for the cover design, website, Instagram, YouTube, and help with so many things!

And finally, thank You, Jesus, for showing us what love looks like and what God the Father is like. You are amazing.

*"Now this is eternal life: that they may know you,*
*the only true God, and Jesus Christ, whom you have sent."*
*John 17:3*

*This is what the Lord says:*
*"Let not the wise boast of their wisdom*
*or the strong boast of their strength*
*or the rich boast of their riches,*
*but let the one who boasts boast about this:*
*that they have the understanding to know me,*
*that I am the Lord, who exercises kindness,*
*justice and righteousness on earth,*
*for in these I delight,"*
*declares the Lord.*
*Jeremiah 9:23-24*

One day I quickly walked into the kitchen from outside the house and slammed the door. I was eighteen and in a rush. My dad burst into an angry flare, yelling at me, "Why are you slamming the door? There is no respect around here!" And off he stormed. A few days later I was with my dad in the kitchen near the same spot, and news just reached him that my two younger brothers, Keith and Neil, had crashed and totaled his car last night while partying with some girls. I looked at my dad waiting for the white heat of rage to explode. To my surprise it didn't come. After exhaling loudly my dad said, "Well, boys will be boys." Then he quietly walked down the hall shaking his head. I was mystified.

Some years later at the age of twenty-three, I had a complete encounter with God. I met with a pastor and told him everything I was doing in college, all the typical stuff with girls and drinking. Additionally I was gut-level honest about some very deep shame issues in my life. After some more conversation, he asked if I wanted to become a Christian and ask Jesus for some real help to change my life. I was shocked to hear myself praying to Jesus out of desperation that things would change. As I left the church, I felt a cleanness that was so beautiful it would be hard to describe. I was also filled with a love that was everything I wanted in life! I was so satisfied that I was overwhelmed!

As the months passed on, it was evident that a new life had indeed been conceived in me. To say that I was completely perfect, however, would be a gross overstatement. But, I was growing. Many things did begin changing in my life, and new compassion, honesty, and goodness began to take shape and spring forth in my relationships and at work. Yet, I began to realize that I had a hard time trusting God when the pressure was on. When I was short on money and didn't know how to pay my bills or college tuition, I struggled to trust that God would help me. When I needed a new job, or needed friends or was worried about those I loved, it was hard to lean on God's goodness.

Over time I realized that I had begun experiencing Jesus' presence and love in some amazing ways and it was really affecting me. However, I also realized that I was always looking backwards over my shoulder, wondering if He would suddenly turn on me and be mean or reject me. I began to realize this was because my dad would be happy one moment and angry a moment later, sometimes boiling over into a complete rage at the slightest thing, like me slamming the door. At other times when I expected him to explode, he would be silent or depressed, like when my brothers destroyed his car. The fact is I could never tell what mood my father would be in. I grew up with that for eighteen years. Sometimes he would get us up in the middle of the night for a "family meeting" and scream at my brothers, my mom, and me for an hour. I didn't understand what the word "manic-depressive" meant, but I knew what it felt like. Friends who had alcoholic dads or moms described similar things.

Now that I was relating to God/Jesus as the primary influencer and authority figure in my life, I simply did not know what to expect. And the stakes were radically higher because I knew that eternal heaven or hell was on the line.

I would have great experiences of God's love as I read the Bible. At other times, though, I would experience great fear as I doubted that He really cared about me. Out of this crucible, I began to pray one prayer in many different forms over and over, "Father God, help me know You. Help me know what You are like. Help me know what You will do and what You will not do. How can I trust You when the pressure is on in life if I don't know what You are like?" I cried out to God for years to "know Him."

I was the one talent man of Matthew 25:24. The owner of the house gave five talents, two talents, and one talent to his servants, potentially equivalent to five, two, and one thousand dollars. The five and two talent servants used the money and made more. The one talent man didn't use his at all because his image of God was warped, distorted, and shot through with raw fear. He said that the master was a "hard" man and that he demanded a harvest without sowing seed. In the NIV Bible the text says that the master repeated the accusations about him back to the man, "So you knew..." but there is a question mark at the end of the text. That means that God is not agreeing with the man's assessment of his character. We miss that often. I surely did! The master was basically saying, "If this is who you thought I was, then shouldn't you have at least put the money in the bank to get me some interest?" The one talent guy wouldn't even lift a finger to do anything. Besides sheer laziness, a big part of the one talent man's problem was his picture of God! He acted out of this fearful and oppressive view of God and, therefore, ran away and did nothing with his one thousand dollars. God wasn't a hard man! In fact, He was very generous. The one talent man could have bought lots of seed with his thousand dollars. So, God had given him the means to plant seeds, in fact tons of seeds! He could have had a huge harvest! Why does the one talent man say, "You gave me no seed?" The one talent man's second accusation against God's character that He demands a harvest without planting seed was an outright lie!

Well, that was my basic view of God, that He was angry and demanding! Yet, nothing could be further from the truth. However, the Holy Spirit began changing my view of God and renewing my mind by having me look at Jesus, now that I was beginning to know Him in a more healthy way. The Holy Spirit was the One at work!

Over time the Holy Spirit would draw my attention to passage after passage in the Bible that showed God's good character. It took years and hundreds of passages to clear my fear-stained image of God and wash it to become cleaner and healthier. My image of God wasn't perfect, but it was becoming healthier than it was. A passage here highlighted Jesus' compassion for the sick. A passage there highlighted Jesus' empathy toward weak humans. Then came the passages where I saw Jesus having patience with Peter's numerous failures and outright sin! As the Spirit brought many passages to light, I began collecting them one by one. I loved the day when I realized Jesus didn't reject Peter when Peter denied Jesus in public. In my mind, this was the ultimate sin. I always wondered what Jesus would do if I were a missionary in a Communist country and they captured me, put a gun to my head, and demanded that I deny knowing Jesus or else they would kill me. I feared that I might crack and deny the Lord. Because I had experienced such anger and rejection from my dad, I was sure God would reject me and send me into the fires of hell. Of course, He didn't do that with Peter, and seeing that was like a fresh warm wind to my fearful heart. Then came the big passages where Jesus got angry. I was terrified of anger. I thought all anger was bad. However, over the months and years, I began to realize Jesus had healthy anger over justice issues. He was mostly angry with the Pharisees, and I could begin to see how they oppressed the poor and everyday uneducated people. I began to appreciate Jesus' anger! I wondered what would've happened, by contrast, if Jesus were spineless and had been passive in moments like that. Maybe some types of anger were good? Seeing the range of Jesus' good character in these many passages began to bring health to my dysfunctional heart and mind.

Trusting God with stressful issues in life was still not easy, but I began to be able to hold onto Him longer and stronger than before, as I saw his good character in Jesus. Now, more than thirty years later, I can look back at a dozen or more journals filled with stories of God's provision when He came through by providing money, friendships, His presence, jobs, or opportunities. I would be lying if I said it was all easy. It wasn't. Growth takes time, effort, and some pain, but it does pay off. I was growing to trust Him more and with bigger and bigger things!

I became convinced that if we will gaze on Jesus, passion will be created in us. We do not rely on our own strength. During the summer of 2014, I got up one morning knowing that I needed to press on with writing this book and engage with several small group studies that were starting in September. However, I had one problem. I had zero motivation or interest in doing any of it. I had no passion for Jesus. My heart was absolutely emotionless. "Hey," I said to myself, "you are writing a whole book on being passionate about Jesus, but your heart is flat, unmoved, and dry! What is your problem? You are the wrong guy to write this book! This is ridiculous!" That is the honest truth. That was my morning. And this wasn't the first day I had felt that way. I was very depressed about this because the dryness and dullness of my heart had been setting in for months.

As September approached, I began pondering, "How am I really going to write more on this book if I am so flat-lined in my heart? How am I going to lead Bible studies on Jesus if this is where I am? This is bad." But on this particular morning, a thought began to dawn on me very gradually. "Chris, this isn't about you. This is about Me. You are not the religious Superman that is always passionate about Me. You never will be. In fact, the real message here is not about you; it's about Me. If regular, every day, one talent passionless people will choose to look at Me and see that I love them, then they will be encouraged and filled with strength to love Me back! I will release passion and power in them bit by bit and day by day." In that moment I realized that my strength, kindness, and desire to do what is good does not originate from myself, but it comes from Jesus. I do have to respond to Him. I'm not saying we can sit back and be passive and watch TV and check Facebook while He does all the work. He initiates, and we respond. However, I was realizing deeply that He is the root of all my goodness. The more I focus on Him, the more I love Him and do the really good things that He commands me to do. Then more of life opens up to be truly abundant!

What you have in your hands is a conversational study on the amazing character of that one unique human being named Jesus and how He relates to us in our sin and failure! As you gaze on the goodness of Jesus, you can understand what God is really like and how He feels about you. Your story, of course, will be different than mine, but your goal will be the same. Choose to look at Jesus, see His goodness, and trust God to transform your heart.

All God's Best!

*Chris Sarris*

P.S. Please don't forget to read the epilogue of this story at the end of this book for the complete picture!

## WHAT IS YOUR IMAGE OF GOD?

As you interact with this study book, honestly ask yourself the question, "What is my image of God?" Be gut-level honest as you answer the questions in this study. This will help you to see where your image of God differs from how God defines Himself. Use the Notes columns and white space in the book to scribble down as many of your thoughts as possible. This is a journey. Write down both sides of your image of God: the dark and fearful side and the light and wonderful side of how you view Him. This is very important because our image of God can come from many different sources. In fact, in our modern culture it is very popular for people to "make up God in their own image." Last time I checked, we were made in His image (Gen 1:26)! However, modern people constantly form their image of God from their own imaginations. What do I mean?

People gather ideas from their own life experiences, parents, bosses, friends' opinions, TV, the internet, and Facebook, and stir them in a pot and out explodes their "idea" of what God is like. And it changes day to day, month to month, and year to year. Do we fully realize what we are doing? This is confusion. We fashion God in our own image through our imagination, and then we pray to it! "God of my imagination, help me!" In the old days people had "physical" idols, and today we have "virtual" idols. There is absolutely no difference. They would carve out a wooden figure and cover it with silver or gold and then fall down before it and pray, "God, save me! Help me!" (Isa 44:16-17). So, if we aren't going to do that, where do we define our image of God? If we don't want to worship our own imagination, where do we look? The solution is to define our image of God based on His terms and His definitions of Himself.

Since we want to relate to God in a healthy way by growing out of dysfunctional, confused, or distorted views of Him, let's dig into what He looks like. Jesus made a profound statement at the end of His life. Some of His very last parting words to His followers were, *"If you have seen me you have seen the Father"* (John 14:9). God has defined Himself by becoming a human being named Jesus. The invisible, uncreated, eternal God is seen perfectly through the visible life of Jesus. Let's avoid the twin pitfalls of picturing God as: (1) harsh, overbearing, and Pharisee-like or (2) overly soft, sissy-like, passive, and filled with cheap grace! The real God is just like Jesus who is the Lion and the Lamb combined in perfect balance (Rev 5:5-6). Let your image of God be based on how He defines Himself as revealed in Jesus. Discover Him more fully in this study!

## WORSHIP WITHOUT MUSIC

This study is different from a regular Bible study - worship is the primary focus of this book. This is a paradigm shift, so keep your eyes on this because it can trip you up. As you study various aspects of Jesus' character, stop frequently and talk to Jesus about Himself. It sounds strange to modern ears, but we want to cultivate worship of the God-Man. Tell Him what you like about Him, what you love about Him, why you are amazed by Him, and what fascinates you about Him! The key is to add devotional conversation with Jesus to your study of the Scriptures. This whole book is really an opportunity to worship Jesus rather than do a mental study exercise in theology. We need excellent theology, but we need to worship the real Jesus even more.

Have you ever considered your prayer time as an opportunity to worship? It is great to use your prayer time for confession of sin and repentance, or for petition or asking for things, but we also want to develop adoration, praise, and delight in Jesus Himself! Connecting with Jesus like the branches to the vine is the issue. What about being fascinated with Jesus in our prayer time and telling Him about it? If I only related to my wife, Kirsty, in terms of confessing what I did wrong and asking for things, she would kill me! (Not really, but you get the idea). That is not a healthy relationship! It is a sick kind of thing posing as a relationship. Connect with Jesus in real terms. Tell Him what you love about Him as you study who He is.

Why call it, "Worship Without Music"? I love music, and I love worshipping with music. However, I don't always have music available, nor do I always have music with the right words that I need. I'm calling it "Worship Without Music" so that we will break out of our typical Sunday morning worship paradigm to engage with worship anytime! If we can experiment and craft worship statements of delight, fascination, and awe to Jesus, we can use these anytime to connect with Him. While commuting to work, at two in the morning to battle anxiety, or on a fifteen-minute walk at lunch to refresh during our work day are all opportunities to feed on Jesus and worship Him. We need to know how to "savor" Him! These worship sections of the book are the "action" sections along with the journaling prompts to help you be more than a spectator reading yet another book. Engage deeply!

Sometimes creating these worship statements directly "to" Jesus (rather than "about" Jesus) can be almost too "personal." Don't let that stop you! My friend Brad says, "Chris, it's 'strangely difficult' to do this." Many find it so. However, if you stick with it, you will find new levels of closeness and intimacy in your relationship with Jesus! Worship is like a rainbow, and it has so many different layers and colors to it. There is the quiet appreciation for who He is, the intense fascination with something unusual that He does, the boisterous praise for His protection of the weak, or the hushed awe of His greatness and power. Explore all of Him in worship!

You can also liken this difference between worshipping Jesus by talking to Him directly, rather than talking about Him, to interacting with someone like an architect. You can talk to an architect and praise the house that he has crafted, the columns, the vaulted ceilings, the curves, and the overall design. But it's an entirely more intimate thing to praise the architect himself. "I've watched how you treat people that work for you, how you engage them with respect and honor. I have also seen how you love your children and treasure your wife. I am greatly impressed with your design skills, but I am even more impressed with who you are and how you treat those around you! I greatly admire you and wish to become like you!" That is what we are after with Jesus!

### WORSHIP FIRST!

Jesus Himself said the first and most important commandment is, *"Love the Lord your God with all your heart and with all your soul and with all your mind and with all your strength"* (Mark 12:29-30). That is the primary subject of this book. Jesus goes on to declare that the second commandment is, *"Love your neighbor as yourself"* (Mark 12:31). I refer continually to these as the first and second commandments. (I'm not referring to the first and second commandments of Moses from the Ten Commandments). Let us not put the second commandment ahead of the first commandment. Let us first worship the living God for all His goodness! Then let us be sure to go on and love our neighbor. Often I find that it is easier to focus on the second commandment rather than the first commandment. Worship can seem nebulous and intangible. Doing things quickly appeals to our task-oriented culture. That is why this book focuses on Jesus' first commandment since it seems to be the more elusive but the more powerful of the two. If you are truly engaging in the first commandment, it will naturally lead to engaging in the second commandment. Worship leads directly into obedience and life application, but we don't rush out of worship to do so. So follow Jesus' first commandment and worship first and worship fully!

### DISCOVERY AND THOUGHTS

Each section is broken up into a "Discovery" section and a "Thoughts" section. In the "Discovery" passages, I put before you events from the four Gospels, ask you to look for Jesus' character, and then have you write down what you see in the blank lines. Be curious and discover what the Holy Spirit will reveal to you before reading my thoughts. This is absolutely critical! I usually cover this material in small groups on online Zoom "discussions." How can I engage that way with you in a book? Therefore, please write down your responses and complete the other half of the conversation. What the Holy Spirit personally shows you will be way more important than anything I have to say. Focus on how Jesus relates to all sorts of different people. In the "Thoughts" section, I compliment your thoughts with some of my thoughts about Jesus' character. All of this is designed to show you Jesus' character more clearly and help you hang onto Him and trust Him, and therefore God, especially during the tough times.

### OLD TESTAMENT LINKS

So many times we have heard people refer to God in the Old Testament as the God of judgment and truth, and Jesus as the God of mercy and grace. There is not a God of the Old Testament that has a different character than the Jesus of the New Testament. They are both the same. God isn't a split personality God. God's character has complete continuity and consistency from Genesis to Revelation. Hebrews 13:8 says, *"Jesus Christ is the same yesterday, today and forever."* Malachi 3:6 says, *"For I am the Lord, I do not change."* The Old Testament passages in the Notes sections, rightly understood, demonstrate the consistency of the God of the Old Testament with Jesus' character in the New Testament. The Old Testament can be very, very confusing to understand because of its ancient culture, customs, and brutal warfare. Hopefully these Old Testament links will help you make some beach-heads or landing zones into seeing that God is just like Jesus even then.

### ADDITIONAL PASSAGES

If you are hungry for more study, look at the additional passages at the back of the book. These illustrate more ways that Jesus relates to the disciples as they mess up. And there are more than these. Take a look through the Gospels and find some others yourself!

### RESOURCES

Please visit our web site at https://GodIsJustLikeJesus.com and particularly look for the link called "The Book" for the latest updates and additional thoughts connected to this book.

If you would like to join an online Zoom discussion covering this book, please email me at Chris@GodIsJustLikeJesus.com.These are the single best ways to process who Jesus is as we discuss together as a community.

You may find our podcasts by searching for "God Is Just Like Jesus" on Apple Podcasts, Spotify, and others. Likewise search on YouTube, Facebook, and Instagram for additional content. Lastly see the "Resources" page at the end of the book for further information.

*And now, let's dig in!*

# JESUS' GOODNESS

## DURING OUR FAILURE AND SIN

---

Throughout this study you will explore the breadth of Jesus' response to the disciples when things went less than perfectly. At the time of writing this, I have found thirty-one times that the disciples screwed up, failed, or sinned. Jesus' response varies from patient instruction, challenge, or correction to discipline.

It is important to note that Jesus dealt very differently with the Pharisees who were not responding to Him than with the disciples who were responding. In fact, the Pharisees hated Him and wanted to murder Him. The more passages you read, the more Jesus' different responses to these two groups becomes apparent. This book is primarily aimed at sincere but imperfect followers of Jesus (there is no other kind of disciple).

Days 1-9 cover a wide spectrum of Jesus' responses to the disciples as they failed and sinned. Days 10-16 cover the final days leading up to the cross and culminating in Jesus' restoration of Peter and the other disciples, as he cooked them breakfast on the beach. Day 16 is the pinnacle of his response to their failure and sin.

As you spend time meditating on these passages, you will realize that Jesus' responses are so good! And, since God is just like Jesus, we can trust that God our Father is relating to us, in our sin and failure, with the same goodness.

So, get ready to worship as you dive into this experience of Jesus' love as He responds to the disciples failures, screw-ups, and outright sins with instruction, challenge, and even correction, yet without the negative responses you might be automatically expecting.

In a word: Worship!

NOTES

*This argument makes me think of Philippians 2:3, "Do nothing out of selfish ambition or vain conceit, but in humility consider others better than yourselves." They are pretty much blowing up this verse head to toe.*

# DAY 1 Discovery

## WHO IS THE GREATEST?

*They left that place and passed through Galilee. Jesus did not want anyone to know where they were, because he was teaching his disciples. He said to them, "The Son of Man is going to be delivered into the hands of men. They will kill him, and after three days he will rise." But they did not understand what he meant and were afraid to ask him about it. They came to Capernaum. When he was in the house, he asked them, "What were you arguing about on the road?" But they kept quiet because on the way they had argued about who was the greatest. Sitting down, Jesus called the Twelve and said, "Anyone who wants to be first must be the very last, and the servant of all." He took a little child whom he placed among them. Taking the child in his arms, he said to them, "Whoever welcomes one of these little children in my name welcomes me; and whoever welcomes me does not welcome me but the one who sent me." Mark 9:30-37*

Describe what is happening between the disciples? What are they doing? Consider Philippians 2:3. How would you have responded to them, if you were Jesus? How does Jesus respond? (Use the Notes section for extra space to write your answers.)

______________________________________________

______________________________________________

### THOUGHTS

I thought this might be a really good event to start the book with! Isn't it interesting to realize that the disciples weren't perfect? In fact, there is no such thing as "Bible people" who get it all absolutely right. There are only "people" who have successes, failures, and sins. We can all take a breath and relax. Jesus knows that weak, imperfect people are the only people who He has to work with.

This passage records the first time the disciples are arguing about which of them is the greatest. It's just good old-fashioned pride and sin! It's just good to call it out so we don't think they were perfect Bible people. Can you imagine some of the things they might be saying? Peter might be saying, "I'm better than all of you because Jesus called me the Rock! And besides that I walked on water!" James might respond, "Honestly, how can you be so arrogant? You sank!" Peter might reply, "Yeah, but I'm the only one that got out of the boat? You guys were too scared!" John might respond, "Well, Jesus called us the Sons of Thunder, so we are clearly the greatest!" Nathaniel might have said, "Yeah, but you tried to wipe out that Samaritan village with a lightning bolt! Jesus rebuked you in front of all of us! And John, you shut down that one guy casting out demons in Jesus' name, and you told him to knock it off. Jesus wasn't real happy about that." A disciple that was not one of the Twelve might have said, "Yeah, I don't think any of you are the greatest. Remember when Jesus was warning us about the yeast of the Pharisees and Sadducees? You all started arguing that it was because we didn't bring any bread. That wasn't what He was talking about at all!"

The disciples know what they are doing is not right because it says that when they came to Capernaum and went into a house, Jesus asks them, "What were you arguing about on the road?" And the text says, "But they kept quiet because on the way they had argued about who was the greatest." Ouch! They know what He is talking about, but they pretend they don't! They are covering over their sin. Isn't it telling that they keep quiet about the whole matter? It is funny in one way, but in another it is serious. They are just like you and me. Have you ever tried to cover up your sin? I have.

However, before we drop off into self-criticism, let's look at how good Jesus' response to them is!

Why do we want to look at this bit of history? Because we are going to see how Jesus deals not with mere failure but outright sin. The disciples are having a serious argument about who is the best, who is greatest, who is the most powerful, or who is the most holy! This is probably arising because Jesus has told them that He will be killed. So they are probably arguing about who will succeed Him as the leader of the movement. And this isn't just a little argument. We have four recorded events in Scripture when this debate erupts! Imagine the twelve most important people at your church having several intense arguments about which of them is the greatest right at the leadership meeting! Imagine them getting really angry. They might be shouting, name-calling, fault-finding, and accusing one another. Or they might be doing it quietly and discreetly but still flexing and throwing their chests out. Imagine them really getting offended. That's what is happening here. It is sin, not just a little argument. This will become clearer as we study the other three times this occurs.

If you were a critical leader or a Pharisee, how would you have reacted? Be honest and write down a few notes. It really helps us grow to process this. Use the line below and the Notes column.

________________________________________________

Also, consider how you talk to yourself when you fail or sin? What do you say to yourself? How do you feel about yourself? What is your attitude toward yourself? Be sure to make notes so that you can really get the most out of this look at Jesus.

________________________________________________

The really important part is Jesus' response. Get this: How does He respond to their failure and sin? It is amazing to realize that He does not respond by accusing them of sin or finding fault with them. Isn't that incredible? He connects with them and urges them to reach higher in life.

**NOTES**

*In Jesus' words, power comes from relationship with Him not from institutions or hierarchy (Pharisee-ism). Corporate businesses teach us the opposite.*

***Old Testament Link***

*Peter wanting to be the greatest and saying the others might fall away reminds me of Joseph with his two dreams of greatness with everyone bowing down to him! Later Joseph brings his father a bad report of his brothers in Genesis 37:2. Jesus instructs Peter, and God deals with Joseph's pride over decades. Genesis 37, 39-45*

**NOTES**

*His patient instruction makes me think of this verse: "His kindness is meant to lead you to repentance." Romans 2:4*

Firstly, He patiently instructs them about being great. He doesn't put down the desire to be great, but He just tells them the best way to go about it, which is through service and humility. Secondly, He takes a little child in His arms and instructs them with a living example of greatness with this little boy or girl. He tells them to become more like a child than a typical adult leader. Jesus is patient with the disciples' failure and outright selfish ambition, and He helps them grow in goodness.

And it is very important to notice that in the face of sin Jesus doesn't get moody. He doesn't get passive-aggressive with them and punish them for hours or days. He doesn't have a melt-down or have an outburst of anger. He is so clean and wholesome in His emotions and response to their sin. He is so wonderfully different than we expect!

Don't you just want to worship Him right now because of who He is?

## TAKEAWAY

*"He who has seen Me has seen the Father" (John 14:9 NASB).*This is our foundational verse! Time and time again, we will look at how Jesus relates to people and connect the dots to realize that this is how God, who is invisible, relates to people. Gazing at Jesus' visible character will help us see God's character.

In this passage, what did you see in Jesus, and what did it reveal to you about God? Secondly, ask yourself, "What does this mean for me?" When you are sinning in competition and pride, how will Jesus and the Father relate to you? Use the lines below and the Notes column to jot down your ideas. Be sure to do this because the ideas the Holy Spirit highlights to you are more important than my thoughts.

________________________________________

________________________________________

For me, Jesus' patient instruction regarding the disciples' sin of competition and strife reveals God's patience as He deals with competition and strife in my life! I love seeing His goodness!

*Website: Look for "The Book" on our website for more Old Testament link information. www.GodIsJustLikeJesus.com*

## FIRST COMMANDMENT PRAYER

Wow, Jesus, it's amazing to understand that Your good character clearly shows me God's character! I love Your patience with the disciples' sin and failure! That gives me confidence that You are not always finding fault with me but You are actually helping me grow in the middle of my sin rather than just tearing me down. You are so different from other people! You are so much better than the enemy of our souls! Your goodness is much better than I have realized!

## WORSHIP WITHOUT MUSIC

Imagine yourself as one of these disciples. Imagine Jesus being patient with your sin and pride. What would you say to Him? Simple worship statements to Jesus can feel awkward at first, but they actually increase your capacity to worship Him. Write down two or three things that you like about Jesus from this passage. Use these starter lines or invent your own:

Jesus, I like the way You________________________________________

______________________________________________________________

Jesus, I'm amazed how You_______________________________________

______________________________________________________________

Invent your own statement of delight:_______________________________

______________________________________________________________

**NOTES**

*Podcasts?*
*Search for "God Is Just Like Jesus" on Apple Podcasts, Spotify, or Amazon Music for the audio version of this series.*

NOTES

THE DISCIPLES HARSHLY CRITICIZE MARY

*Six days before the Passover, Jesus came to Bethany, where Lazarus lived, whom Jesus had raised from the dead. Here a dinner was given in Jesus' honor. Martha served, while Lazarus was among those reclining at the table with him. Then Mary took about a pint of pure nard, an expensive perfume; she poured it on Jesus' feet and wiped his feet with her hair. And the house was filled with the fragrance of the perfume. But one of his disciples, Judas Iscariot, who was later to betray him, objected, "Why wasn't this perfume sold and the money given to the poor? It was worth a year's wages." He did not say this because he cared about the poor but because he was a thief; as keeper of the money bag, he used to help himself to what was put into it. "Leave her alone," Jesus replied. "It was intended that she should save this perfume for the day of my burial. You will always have the poor among you, but you will not always have me." John 12:1-8*

*Some of those present were saying indignantly to one another, "Why this waste of perfume? It could have been sold for more than a year's wages and the money given to the poor." And they rebuked her harshly. Mark 14:4-5*

*Aware of this, Jesus said to them, "Why are you bothering this woman? She has done a beautiful thing to me. The poor you will always have with you, but you will not always have me. When she poured this perfume on my body, she did it to prepare me for burial. Truly I tell you, wherever this gospel is preached throughout the world, what she has done will also be told, in memory of her." Then one of the Twelve–the one called Judas Iscariot–went to the chief priests and asked, "What are you willing to give me if I deliver him over to you?" Matt 26:10-14*

Describe what is happening here in your own words? Who is accusing Mary? (There is more than one person.) Why are they finding fault with her? Is there more going on here than just lust for money? What event in Mary's life has just occurred previously? (Hint: John 11). What does Jesus do for Mary regarding the attack and criticism?

____________________________________________________________

____________________________________________________________

## THOUGHTS

Interestingly, we find out where Jesus wants to be during His last week before He dies. Jesus wants to be with His good friends Mary, Martha, and Lazarus, whom He has recently raised from the dead (John 11). Perhaps He wants to be around people He loves deeply? They would be eternally lost if He didn't complete His mission on the cross. Mary goes all out and cracks open a jar of expensive perfume that was her

NOTES

inheritance and possible means for daily life. She lavishes it all on Jesus! In the past she has sat at the feet of Jesus and received all that He has said. She has delighted in Jesus. Now, recently, Jesus has raised her brother Lazarus from the dead, and she is overwhelmed with adoration and worship! Judas snaps. Suddenly, Judas gets really angry and accuses Mary of wasting the money in front all the disciples. All he can see is the "wasted" money. He can't see Jesus. It is a clear example of what Jesus said in Matthew 6:24, *"You cannot serve both God and money."* Why? Because you will ultimately value one over the other. One will be subordinated or serve the other. Judas does not value the One Mary values. Judas cannot see or perceive Jesus in all His wonder and goodness because he lusts for human money and what it can get him. He has missed what Jesus can give him. Can you imagine Judas was not deeply touched as he saw Jesus heal the suffering, restore sight to the blind, clean the lepers, and raise the dead to return them to their mother or father? Additionally, Judas has been stealing from the money that people had given Jesus to feed and house Him as He traveled through Israel. It's hard to understand such a soul.

The Gospel of Mark says that Judas and some other disciples were indignantly criticizing Mary between themselves. It's important to know that it wasn't just Judas. Some of the others joined in accusing her. It says they rebuked her "harshly." The Message Bible says, *"They swelled up in anger, nearly bursting with indignation over her"* (Mark 14:5). Can you imagine it? Judas leads the way, but Peter, James, John, or some of the others got involved in a pretty severe criticism storm over Mary. Can you imagine it? It is just sin.

Let's consider another reason Judas, in particular, is attacking Mary. Matthew 26:14 reveals that right after this event Judas goes to the Pharisees to betray Jesus. Why? There is something about Mary's wonderful love and extravagant worship of Jesus that throws Judas over the edge. It's too much for him. Judas hasn't delighted in Jesus as I mentioned. The people's confusion and suffering don't touch him. Judas hasn't celebrated Lazarus' return to his sisters who were deeply grieving. Since he hasn't given his heart over to people or Jesus in this way, there is something about Mary's wild abandoned worship of Jesus that offends Judas at a deep level. Judas doesn't deeply love or value Jesus.

I think it is important to note that Mary isn't doing this because she is trying to be "dedicated to the Lord." There is no religion here but true faith and worship. She knows how dedicated Jesus is to her. She knows how much Jesus loves her. She has been opening her heart to receive all of God's love through Jesus, and now she is merely loving Him back! Mary has been drinking regularly from that Spring of Living Water that Jesus talked about to the Samaritan woman (John 4:14) and that He told the crowds about at the Feast of Tabernacles (John 7:38). She has been reconnecting to the Tree of Life (Gen 2:9; Rev 22:2). So often in life, we can get this reversed, we can think "we" have to love Him first, and then He will love us back. It's not true! First, we need to receive God's love, and then we will love Him back in full devotion. And secondly, we give that love to others by caring for them. This is what 1 John 4:19 says,

**NOTES**

**Old Testament Link**
Judas' attacking Mary reminds me of King Saul attacking David. Jesus rebukes Judas and the others and instructs them. Saul sends the companies of soldiers to apprehend David, and the Holy Spirit subdues them all.

*"We love because He first loved us."*

Additionally, Mary is completely disconnected from the argument about which of them is the greatest. In fact, she embodies Jesus' words about those who are the greatest should serve others. She is serving Jesus with all that she has!

Jesus praises Mary on multiple fronts, *"She has done a beautiful thing to me"* (Mark 14:6). Wow, what does it take for the eternal Son of God to say that a thing done to Him by a human is "beautiful"? It is high praise for Mary. Then Jesus continues praising her saying, *"Truly I tell you, wherever this gospel is preached throughout the world, what she has done will also be told, in memory of her"* (Mark 16:9). Wow, Jesus sets up a lasting memorial to Mary! That is incredible! It is lavish praise from the wonderful One for a human who is devoted to Him but far from perfect.

In addition to Jesus praising Mary, we should call out His wonderful protection for her! What does Jesus do? How does He relate to Judas and the other disciples that are attacking Mary? First, He drops His shield of protection over Mary, *"Why are you bothering this woman?"* He rebukes Judas and any others who are in agreement with him. They are dragging her through the mud and Jesus drops His shield of protection over her! One person said, "Mary is giving Jesus all she has! She is giving Him her inheritance and money. She is giving her heart to Him in radical vulnerability and pure intimacy! She gladly spends herself on the wonderful One!" It's awesome to see Jesus receive such a visceral heart-level gift, protect her vulnerability, and greatly praise and extol her for all the ages to come! Wow, He is magnificent!

Lastly, how does Jesus deal with Judas and the other disciples? Look at what He says and does. He uses a combination of instruction, challenge, and correction without rejection. He corrects by saying, *"Why are you bothering this woman?"* Then He instructs them with, *"She has done a beautiful thing to Me."* And He continues by stating, *"Wherever this gospel is preached throughout the world, what she has done will also be told...."* Jesus doesn't go passive and avoid the issue but hits it head on. However, He doesn't use their unclean motivation methods of fault-finding, accusation, and criticism. Jesus employs clean instruction, challenge, and correction to motivate clean growth. It seems unusual to say, but Jesus is emotionally healthy!

## TAKEAWAY

*"The Son is the image of the invisible God"* (Col 1:15). Since Jesus is the image of God, write down some ideas on the line below and in the Notes column related to what Jesus shows you about God. Also, ask yourself, "What does this mean for me?" What about when you are being criticized by someone? Or when you are criticizing someone else?

---

This is an amazing and deep passage that reveals tons about Jesus. He protects and praises Mary which reveals that God protects and praises Mary. However, at the same time He instructs, challenges, and corrects Judas and the other disciples without rejection, which reveals the Father's instruction, challenge, and correction without rejection. Jesus is emotionally healthy and wonderfully balanced, and that reveals God's emotional health and balance. As we worship Him, we become more like Him.

## FIRST COMMANDMENT PRAYER

Jesus, I love how healthy You are! I love how You protect Mary and how You praise her! I never thought of You praising or complimenting anyone. Thank You for showing me Your goodness. I also like that You instruct Judas and the other disciples. You correct them, but without rejection! That is amazing to me given how my dad related to me. That really helps bring my fear down and enables me to draw closer to You rather than running away. I can see myself growing from Your challenge and correction rather than just shutting down. You're amazing!

## WORSHIP WITHOUT MUSIC

Look at how Jesus has treated Mary and start crafting some statements of enjoyment and delight directly to Him (rather than about Him). Then look at how He relates to the disciples and write some other statements to Him. Use the prompts below or cross them out and use your own words.

Jesus, I like how You ______________________________

Jesus, I love how You ______________________________

Jesus, Your ______________________________ is amazing!

**NOTES**

*Online Discussions: Consider joining a weekly Online Discussion to read and discuss passages about Jesus with a community. Look for "Online Discussions" on the website.*

NOTES

THE DISCIPLES ARE CONFUSED

*"Listen! A farmer went out to sow his seed. As he was scattering the seed, some fell along the path, and the birds came and ate it up. Some fell on rocky places, where it did not have much soil. It sprang up quickly, because the soil was shallow. But when the sun came up, the plants were scorched, and they withered because they had no root. Other seed fell among thorns, which grew up and choked the plants, so that they did not bear grain. Still other seed fell on good soil. It came up, grew and produced a crop, some multiplying thirty, some sixty, some a hundred times." Then Jesus said, "Whoever has ears to hear, let them hear." When he was alone, the Twelve and the others around him asked him about the parables. Mark 4:3-10*

*His disciples asked him what this parable meant. He said...."This is the meaning of the parable...." Luke 8:9,11*

It's always so good to know I'm not the only one confused by Jesus. So were the disciples!

What do you feel as you see the disciples struggling with confusion over what Jesus said? Can you relate as you have read the Bible? Do you think this is the only time this occurred? Jesus' response to their confusion is very simple; try to put it into words. Describe what Jesus doesn't do and what He does do. Contrast that to how you imagine other people or the Pharisees might respond to their disciples' confusion.

See Matthew 13:36 for another time the disciples were confused!

________________________________________________

________________________________________________

### THOUGHTS

Look at the Additional Study Passages for two more examples of the disciples being confused by Jesus' teaching.

You might think this passage is an unusual and possibly uninteresting place to look at Jesus' character. However, it reveals so much about Him. I love seeing that the Bible is honest enough to reveal the disciples' failures and outright sins! That is one of a hundred reasons that convinces me the Bible is true and accurately records history as it occurred. No one writing a book in the Old World would have included so many failures of God's best people in both the Old Testament and the New Testament, unless it just happened time and time again. Someone inventing a story would have polished it all up and made the heroes of faith look a lot better. In this specific case, the Bible reveals how confused the disciples were. Don't for a minute imagine that the disciples understood everything Jesus said or did. This happened on many different occasions and different situations. It is good to know we aren't the only ones confused by what Jesus says or does. This really helps me because I have been confused by the Bible many times since I began reading it thirty years ago! It is good to realize that Jesus doesn't expect 100 percent understanding right from the start nor during our thirtieth, fiftieth, or eightieth year of living! However, what is even greater is that the Bible reveals Jesus' wonderful response to those who are responding to Him when they are confused. Simply put, Jesus patiently and kindly instructs His followers. I don't think this point can be overstated to humans who are generally deeply insecure about their connection with God, the Father.

As we look at the passage, we see Jesus telling the parable of the four soils. There are seeds, rocky soil, weeds, and good soil. What is going on here? The disciples simply don't get it. They come to Jesus and ask Him what the parable means. I love this because it reveals that they felt secure enough with Jesus that they could ask Him for help. They could admit that they didn't understand - that they weren't perfect. Jesus is the kind of person who makes room for learning and growing. Does that surprise you? Sometimes during Bible studies people don't speak up because they are afraid someone will look down on them or criticize them. How does Jesus respond? In delightful simplicity, He patiently instructs them. It's almost so simple you could overlook His kindness and goodness. You don't hear many sermons on this; however, if you digest it, you will find a new joy and security springing up in your connection with Him. You will find a new openness to ask Him the questions that you want to ask, knowing He will patiently instruct you and lead you to a deeper relationship with the Father.

And get this, Jesus doesn't find fault with them. Jesus doesn't criticize them. Often we are aware that Jesus challenges the disciples, the crowds, and the Jewish leaders. But how often do we look for and appreciate one of His most frequent characteristics, that of patient instruction? The more you look for this in Scripture, the more you will see it emerge. It is one of the most basic things Jesus does and all without the typical fault-finding and criticism that can accompany some teachers. Have you ever felt embarrassed to ask a Bible question because the leader might look down on you? Jesus does none of that. You will find that He is emotionally healthy. Here we get a clear picture of Jesus' straightforward instruction!

## TAKEAWAY

*"The Son is the radiance of God's glory and the exact representation of His being..."* (Heb 1:3). Since Jesus is the exact representation of God, what did you see in Him that revealed something new in God that you never saw before? What does this suggest for you? Have you ever been confused by the Bible? Or something the Holy Spirit has said to you? Use the line below and the Notes column for your insights.

---

What I saw was Jesus' patient instruction, without finding fault in them, during their confusion. This revealed to me God's patience without fault-finding as He deals with the confusion in my life. Imagine if everyone in the world knew this about God? Everyone would feel free to ask God questions to help them live life! If we would all expect insight and help from God rather than fearing other responses, the world would be a different place. He is amazing!

## NOTES

*I never thought of Jesus as "patient."*

**Old Testament Link**

*This reminds me of the prophet Samuel's confusion over which of Jesse's sons to anoint as king. God perfectly instructs Samuel without fault-finding or accusation. 1 Samuel 16:1-13 especially v.7*

NOTES

*YouTube:*
*Search for "God Is Just Like Jesus" on YouTube for this series and other videos.*

FIRST COMMANDMENT PRAYER

Father, I love knowing that Your desire is to deliver human beings from confusion and darkness. You know that we are deeply confused about Your good character. We doubt You and fear You because we can't clearly see who You are. Thank You for sending Jesus to reveal that You patiently instruct us to grow us up into Your own goodness for our joy and peace!

### WORSHIP WITHOUT MUSIC

Simply write down two or three things you like about Jesus' response to the disciples' confusion. Use our starter suggestions or write your own here or in the Notes column.

Jesus, I like Your ______________________________

Jesus, it's really wonderful that You ______________________________

Jesus, Your ______________________________ is so good!

Take the last three days of Worship Without Music and go walk for fifteen minutes, telling Him all the things you like about and love about Him. Writing your favorites on a 3 x 5 card or putting them into an email to view on your phone is a great way to take them with you. Alternatively, journal "to" Him for fifteen minutes or create art with your worship! Choose the way you most easily and freely worship Him.

## NOTES

Use this page as extra space for your notes and thoughts.

NOTES

# DAY 4
## Discovery

ARE JAMES AND JOHN THE GREATEST?

*They were on their way up to Jerusalem, with Jesus leading the way, and the disciples were astonished, while those who followed were afraid. Again he took the Twelve aside and told them what was going to happen to him. "We are going up to Jerusalem," he said, "and the Son of Man will be delivered over to the chief priests and the teachers of the law. They will condemn him to death and will hand him over to the Gentiles, who will mock him and spit on him, flog him and kill him. Three days later he will rise." Then James and John, the sons of Zebedee, came to him. "Teacher," they said, "we want you to do for us whatever we ask." "What do you want me to do for you?" he asked. They replied, "Let one of us sit at your right and the other at your left in your glory." "You don't know what you are asking," Jesus said. "Can you drink the cup I drink or be baptized with the baptism I am baptized with?" "We can," they answered. Jesus said to them, "You will drink the cup I drink and be baptized with the baptism I am baptized with, but to sit at my right or left is not for me to grant. These places belong to those for whom they have been prepared." When the ten heard about this, they became indignant with James and John. Jesus called them together and said, "You know that those who are regarded as rulers of the Gentiles lord it over them, and their high officials exercise authority over them. Not so with you. Instead, whoever wants to become great among you must be your servant, and whoever wants to be first must be slave of all. For even the Son of Man did not come to be served, but to serve, and to give his life as a ransom for many." Mark 10:32-45*

*It was about that time that the mother of the Zebedee brothers came with her two sons and knelt before Jesus with a request. "What do you want?" Jesus asked. She said, "Give your word that these two sons of mine will be awarded the highest places of honor in your kingdom, one at your right hand, one at your left hand." Matt 20:20-21 (MSG)*

*When the ten others heard about this, they lost their tempers, thoroughly disgusted with the two brothers. So Jesus got them together to settle things down. Matt 20:24 (MSG)*

I think I might answer Jesus' question a little more slowly and thoughtfully!

What are James, John, and their mom trying to do? How does Jesus respond to them? Contrast Jesus' response to how other people might respond. What does Jesus say to all the disciples? What does that show you about His character?

No wonder our pastors and leaders have so many issues leading us. They (and we) are as imperfect and fraught with pride as the twelve disciples, until Jesus instructs, corrects, and matures us!

____________________________________________

____________________________________________

### THOUGHTS

Here we are again. The disciples are fighting and striving among themselves to be first! They want to lord their position over others; they want to be the CEO of the company and be on top of the food chain! Imagine them trying to plot and maneuver to get the highest position. If you saw this in a person, what would you say?

A legalistic pastor or preacher might say, "Wow, you guys are so fleshly! You are so worldly! What blatant sin! You can't be on my leadership team! You're not holy enough." That is what is really happening here. James and John are trying to sneak in, with their mother's help, to squeeze past Peter and the other nine and grab the throne to the right and left of the God-Man, Jesus! Now, get this. This event occurs in Matthew 18. Do you remember what happened in Matthew 17? Right? It was the Mount of Transfiguration where Jesus' hidden identity is revealed to Peter, James, and John. Guess who shows up to talk to Jesus about His departure or crucifixion? None other than Moses and Elijah! So, if we do the math, James and John are saying essentially, "We appreciate Moses and Elijah. I mean, they are awesome! But we still think we deserve the right and left of your throne, Jesus. They can be number three and four after us!" These guys are trying to squeeze past two of the greatest prophets who have ever lived, not to mention all the other disciples!

I'm not sure I know what to say (mic drop).

Another fascinating thing is James and John think that if they ask Jesus first, they will get the highest reward of heaven, which is stunning because in a way it reveals how approachable Jesus was. A Pharisee would have torn them to shreds verbally! I think the other ten disciples are hacked off because they also know how approachable Jesus is and are possibly thinking, "Dang, they asked first! He will probably give it to them!"

Regardless, they are really sinning in selfish ambition! Again, in Philippians 2:3, Paul clearly speaks to this issue head on, *"Do nothing out of selfish ambition or vain conceit, but in humility consider others better than yourselves."* Wow! The disciples were really getting into trouble here! There is raw pride and insecurity at the core of such contention. My friend Brian said, "They might just be interested in riding Jesus' coattails to glory!"

Ready for a few more imaginary arguments between the disciples? If not, flip the page. Peter might have started again, "I'm still the greatest. I was the one who first figured out that Jesus was the Messiah! I also figured out that He was God's own Son. Jesus called me the 'Rock'! He said He would build His church on me! Get it?" They might have responded, "Peter, you couldn't even understand the parable about eating and what makes a person clean or unclean. Jesus called you 'dull.' We are pretty sure you're not the greatest." Judas might chime in, "Clearly I'm the greatest because Jesus trusts me with all the money!" James and John might have said, "We were with Jesus on the mountain top when He was totally transformed into His divine self!" Peter: "Yeah, I was there too!" They might have responded, "But you started babbling on about what you could do, getting all the attention on yourself, and it shut down the whole supernatural encounter!" And so the arguments could go.

Why is it important to process this kind of sin with the detail we are giving it? We need to see the depth in which the disciples are "walking in the flesh" to understand, by contrast, the beautiful character of Jesus. Remember, the disciples are the future

## NOTES

*They are wanting position to "lord it" over the others.*

*The more we know God really loves us, we will run to Him instead of from Him when we sin.*

***Old Testament Link***
*James and John clutching for power reminds me of Jacob who wanted to be the greatest and coveted Esau's birthright and Esau's blessing from Isaac as the firstborn. God deals with Jacob's sin through the dream at Bethel, through Laban's oppression, and wrestling with God/Jesus in the night. It's all instruction and correction without rejection. Genesis 25-33*

NOTES

leadership of Jesus' church. For a regular human leader, it would be cause for great discouragement and even despair if his young protégés were not ready for their assigned roles. They are violating one of the core principles of the movement - namely, service and humility. Jesus has called them to be servant leaders, and they are failing miserably at their core function! (Ouch! That's sensitive!)

Secondly, we need to understand the imperfections and sins of the disciples relative to Jesus' patient response so that when we fail and sin, we can hear Jesus' patient response toward us! That will strengthen us to grow in goodness, rather than being overwhelmed by the Devil's condemnation for failure and sin which makes us want to quit and give up!

Notice how intense this debate is. Mark 10:41 says that, when the ten heard about James' and John's request, they were indignant. This word means furious, hacked off, angry, fuming, irate, and livid among other synonyms. The parallel passage (Matt 20:25) in the Message Bible says, *"When the 10 heard about this, they lost their tempers, thoroughly disgusted with the two brothers."* However, what does Jesus do when He sees the anger and division in the disciples?

---

Amazingly, Jesus calls them all together and rounds them up. They have divided into two groups. Talk about the original church split! "James and John, come over here. Peter, Matthew, Thomas, and the rest of you guys, come over here too. We are going to talk about this" (my paraphrase). Then Jesus basically instructs them, again! He teaches them how to be great by being humble and serving one another. Get it? Jesus is patient once again. This is the second time. You might think He would be getting a little angry in an unclean way like I would. You might think He would be getting a little hot. But He is not. It is the Holy Spirit's fruit of patience all over again.

If you think of God as harsh and authoritarian, you will not be able to be honest, extend yourself, and risk in the kingdom because you will fear being beaten down. No one risks in front of a true Pharisee. However, if you see that God is just like Jesus, you have the room and acceptance to risk for the kingdom and step out in faith, even if you might fail. Again, having our image of God cleaned up and healed is what empowers the one talent man of Matthew 25:24 to let go of fear and start to trust God and therefore start using his one talent to care about others and the world!

I'll just finish with this. If the disciples had figured this out quickly and become these incredibly humble servants, the world would surely be a better place. However, I would feel like a loser, because it has taken me such a long time to grow in even a little bit of this. I also would not have seen Jesus' goodness and patient instruction in the Scriptures! So, I'm grateful for His redemption

NOTES

TAKEAWAY

*"The one who looks at me is seeing the one who sent me"* (John 12:45). Ok, given that if you see Jesus you are seeing the One who sent Him, what did He just reveal to you about God? Secondly, what is the significance for you when you see your own repetitive sins in pride and arrogance?

---

Jesus' patience and instruction to James and John and the other ten during their sin reveals God's patience and instruction for the weak and imperfect followers even when it is the second time they argue out of competition and pride!

FIRST COMMANDMENT PRAYER

Jesus, You are the exact picture of God! You are amazing! It is wonderful that You are patient with James and John as they are filled with selfish ambition, trying to grab the highest level of honor in Your kingdom. I love the way You gather the ten back together with James and John, and patiently instruct them about their sin. I love You because You don't accuse them or reject them but You grow them up! You are the Wonderful Counselor of Isaiah 9:6!

*For Frequently Asked Questions see FAQ's on our website under "The Book" www.GodIsJustLikeJesus.com*

WORSHIP WITHOUT MUSIC

Have you ever been in a situation at work or church where you were pushing for a new position or promotion that you thought you deserved? Did those in authority around you deal with you as gracefully as Jesus did with His disciples?

Jesus, I'm amazed by Your ______________________

Jesus, I love Your ______________________

Invent your own: ______________________

NOTES

I wonder what made Peter say that?

It's actually a huge success that Peter had great faith and could walk on water. None of the others got out of the boat.

# DAY 5
## Discovery

PETER WALKS ON WATER AND THEN SINKS

*Immediately Jesus made the disciples get into the boat and go on ahead of him to the other side, while he dismissed the crowd. After he had dismissed them, he went up on a mountainside by himself to pray. Later that night, he was there alone, and the boat was already a considerable distance from land, buffeted by the waves because the wind was against it. Shortly before dawn Jesus went out to them, walking on the lake. When the disciples saw him walking on the lake, they were terrified. "It's a ghost," they said, and cried out in fear. But Jesus immediately said to them: "Take courage! It is I. Don't be afraid." "Lord, if it's you," Peter replied, "tell me to come to you on the water." "Come," he said. Then Peter got down out of the boat, walked on the water and came toward Jesus. But when he saw the wind, he was afraid and, beginning to sink, cried out, "Lord, save me!" Immediately Jesus reached out his hand and caught him. "You of little faith," he said, "why did you doubt?" And when they climbed into the boat, the wind died down. Then those who were in the boat worshiped him, saying, "Truly you are the Son of God." Matt 14:22-33*

*He cried, "Master, save me!" Jesus didn't hesitate. He reached down and grabbed his hand. Then he said, "Faint-heart, what got into you?" Matt 14:30-31 (MSG)*

How does Jesus treat Peter after he fails to keep walking on the water? What does Jesus do the instant Peter starts to sink?

________________________________________

________________________________________

Let's ask a few more questions. Provide your honest answers in the blanks.

Does Jesus reject Peter for sinking in the water either personally or relative to His leadership position? Personal rejection would be something like, "Peter, I don't want to hang out with you anymore." Positional rejection would be something like, "Peter, you can no longer be a leader in My church." Explain why or why not. To support your position, use other events from the Gospels.

________________________________________

________________________________________

________________________________________

Think about what we have seen in Jesus so far. Does Jesus kick Peter off the leadership team for: (1) not understanding a parable, (2) for not having "great faith" but only "little faith," or (3) for failing to continue to walk on water?

---

What is the difference between challenging someone and rejecting someone? What is the difference between an athletic coach who constantly criticizes a track runner's or football player's faults and openly mocks them in front of the team and a coach who intensely challenges and corrects the same athlete to do better and work harder because he sees their potential and wants them to be great? The same questions also applies to managers in corporate America and pastors of churches. Comment on any of the three environments. Use the Notes column for extra space.

---

---

How does it make you feel when you see that Peter can fail in different ways and Jesus does not reject him? Jesus may instruct Peter, or even correct Peter, but He never rejects Peter. What does that mean to you?

---

---

## THOUGHTS

Here we have a different water and boat scene than the furious storm that Jesus calms in Day 10. Jesus has just fed the crowd of 5,000 men (probably 15,000 or more men, women, and children altogether). Jesus tells the disciples to get in the boat and go ahead of Him across the Sea of Galilee. He stays behind and goes up a mountain and prays to His Father. Jesus can see the disciples straining at the oars (Mark 6:48). Between three and six in the morning (fourth watch of the night), Jesus walks down the mountain, puts His feet on the water, and starts walking out to the disciples who were in the middle of the lake. It was about three miles out onto the lake (John 6:19). When the disciples see Him, they are terrified! They think He is a ghost or a spirit without a physical human body. Jesus calms their terror. (How would you feel?) Jesus basically says, "Take courage! It is Me!" Interestingly, Peter has learned to trust Jesus more fully since the furious storm incident. Peter says to Jesus, "If that is You, then tell me to come out on the water with You!" (my paraphrase). Jesus says one word (possibly with the hint of a smile), "Come!" Peter is exhibiting some real faith in Jesus. Notice, none of the other disciples went out on the water, not even James or John.

## NOTES

*I love seeing Peter's successes as well as his failures.*

*I love how Jesus grabs Peter so quickly.*

*My image of God was so distorted and warped that I interpreted, "Why did you doubt?" with so much fear, accusation and rejection, until I thoroughly studied Jesus' character. No wonder I was so afraid of God!*

**NOTES**

But Peter does a great thing! He is putting one foot after another on the surface of the waves! He is really doing it! He is walking toward Jesus, apparently looking at Him the whole time. This is amazing! Peter has a huge success! However, a little bit later he takes his eyes off Jesus and becomes filled with fear as he focuses on the blowing wind and the crashing waves. Peter begins to sink! The text says that, *"Immediately Jesus reached out His hand and caught him"*. This is Jesus' protection, which might have been one of the characteristics you listed. It is awesome to see Jesus' protection, especially in the middle of failure! That gives us a lot of confidence in Him! We expect His protection when we are succeeding, but it is even more powerful when we are failing or sinning! (Think about the woman caught in adultery that the Pharisees bring to Jesus in John 8. Jesus essentially protects her in the middle of their accusation and her sin. Pretty awesome!)

Then Jesus utters a question, *"You of little faith...why did you doubt?"* Remember that our culture is saturated with accusation and fault-finding. People accuse the government. People accuse each other. The news relentlessly accuses everyone! People accuse themselves. We find fault with everything around us and complain often. However, try to strip this out of your image of Jesus and then only think about Him. If you are prone to accusation (and we all are), you will read those feelings into Jesus' question. Remember the enemy wants to masquerade his voice as God's voice. He is always trying to lace accusation and condemnation into our feelings. However, Romans 8:1 clearly says, *"There is no condemnation for those who are in Christ."* So don't go there so quickly when you think of Jesus!

Let's focus on Jesus' healthy methods of motivation like encouragement, patient instruction, healthy challenge, correction without rejection, and wholesome discipline for our good growth.

After reading and re-reading many passages about Jesus' attitude when the disciples fail and sin, I have come to the conclusion that Jesus is instructing and challenging Peter for his growth in this passage. In the past when my image of God was saturated with accusation and condemnation, I always interpreted Jesus as criticizing Peter, finding fault with him, and condemning him for failure. Now I know that Jesus is doing something completely different. I realized that Jesus is teaching Peter that he didn't actually have to doubt. I love how the Message Bible puts it, *"Faint-heart, what got into you?"* Beautiful! That was much more accessible for me!

*As we worship Jesus, we become more like Him. Law and rules don't transform us into His image like fascination and worship do.*

I also think He is challenging Peter to stay more focused on Him next time. You can read that question, *"You of little faith...why did you doubt?"* many different ways. It all depends on how you see Jesus and your image of God. When you study all of the Gospels and Jesus' good character in many different events, I believe it becomes clearer that instruction and challenge are the predominate characteristics here!

Let's contrast Jesus' character to that of the Devil. It is clear that Jesus does NOT use the Devil's unhealthy motivation. Jesus does not use disappointment: "Wow, I am sooooo disappointed in you, Peter! Will you ever get it together and learn how to obey me?" Jesus does NOT cross his arms on His chest and use passive aggression, "Maybe this could be a little lesson, Peter." Jesus does NOT fly off the handle and use accusation or fault-finding like the Devil would, "Couldn't you have just kept your eyes on me? What a loser!" Jesus does NOT motivate with rejection. "If you don't walk on water the whole way next time, I just might not reach down and grab you!" These are unhealthy methods of motivation. Unfortunately, we all have used these ourselves or had them used on us. We have also had parents, leaders, and pastors use these unhealthy motivations against us as well. How many of us are wounded because pastors have not been properly fathered or mothered and they have preached and given us an image of God that is filled with unhealthy motivation methods? However, Jesus doesn't do any of that. Jesus isn't dysfunctional; He is healthy! Since we see something different in Jesus, we can turn and reach for greater emotional health!

Rather, we can read these words of Jesus knowing that He isn't accusing or condemning Peter or us for our failures. We know that He went to the cross to save us and Peter. Jesus is for us! So we can read these words in a healthy way. Jesus is saying something like, "Don't take your eyes off Me in the storms of life! You can do this. Focus! You don't have to doubt. You can maintain faith in Me. I will help you!" (my paraphrase). Jesus loves Peter by instructing and challenging Peter to grow! It is the goodness of Jesus growing Peter to be the healthy man and leader he is called to be! As Ephesians 2:10 says, *"For we are God's workmanship, created in Christ Jesus to do good works."* Peter is Jesus' workmanship, and He cares for Peter and is trying to build him up for Peter's good and the good of the sheep he will feed.

The ultimate call on Peter's life and ours is not to become leaders on large platforms disseminating theological information, but to enter the truly high calling of becoming mothers and fathers in the lives of many in the kingdom!

### TAKEAWAY

*"Anyone who has seen me has seen the Father"* (John 14:9). The verse says that as we look at Jesus we can see God. What have you just seen in Jesus as He relates to Peter that shows you something new about who God is? Have you ever dared to do something great only to halfway succeed and then fail in the end? How does Jesus and the Father relate to you?

---

Jesus' protection and healthy challenge to Peter to grow in faith reveal the Father's protection and healthy challenge to call us higher in faith and trust. He only motivates us in healthy ways!

## NOTES

**Old Testament Link**

This reminds me of Gideon struggling to obey God. He wrestles with fear, saying, "My clan's the weakest and I'm the least." Then he asks God for two signs. Peter walks on water and then has fear. Gideon has fear but afterwards has success. God instructs Gideon as He does Peter, with words and signs.

Judges 6:13-40

NOTES

## FIRST COMMANDMENT PRAYER

When I see how You relate to Peter in his failures and sins, I get a picture of how You relate to me in my failures and sins! I love how You immediately grab Peter when he's sinking! Help me remember when You have done this in my life, then I can turn to You and grow, rather than fear You and reject myself for my sins. That mindset actually keeps me trapped in my sins. I love how You call Peter higher but without rejection. I always want to run to You rather than from You when I sin – so that I can grow in goodness! You care for us better than we care for ourselves!

### WORSHIP WITHOUT MUSIC

What do you enjoy or like about Jesus in this passage? He's here. He's with you. Write two or three simple, child-like, worship statements "to" Him rather than about Him. If the starter statements are helpful, go back to Days 1-4 and use some of those.

Jesus, I love the way You______________________________

Invent your own:

________________________________________

________________________________________

*If you are interested in a deep-dive online seminar, look at the website for "Online Seminars."*

## NOTES

Use this page as extra space for your notes and thoughts.

NOTES

Wow, Peter is so honest about what he really feels. I bet Jesus was way more **approachable** than we know or else Peter could never have asked the question.

It's amazing! Jesus is so patient!

# DAY 6
## Discovery

PETER WORRIES ABOUT HIS SACRIFICE

*Then Jesus said to his disciples, "Truly I tell you, it is hard for someone who is rich to enter the kingdom of heaven. Again I tell you, it is easier for a camel to go through the eye of a needle than for someone who is rich to enter the kingdom of God." When the disciples heard this, they were greatly astonished and asked, "Who then can be saved?" Jesus looked at them and said, "With man this is impossible, but with God all things are possible." Peter answered him, "We have left everything to follow you! What then will there be for us?" Jesus said to them, "Truly I tell you, at the renewal of all things, when the Son of Man sits on his glorious throne, you who have followed me will also sit on twelve thrones, judging the twelve tribes of Israel. And everyone who has left houses or brothers or sisters or father or mother or wife or children or fields for my sake will receive a hundred times as much and will inherit eternal life. But many who are first will be last, and many who are last will be first." Matt19:23-30*

*The disciples were staggered. "Then who has any chance at all?" Jesus looked hard at them and said, "No chance at all if you think you can pull it off yourself. Every chance in the world if you trust God to do it." Then Peter chimed in, "We left everything and followed you. What do we get out of it?" Matt 19:25-27 (MSG)*

How does Peter feel? What is he worrying about? How would some leaders have responded to Peter? How does Jesus respond to Peter's exasperated question?

________________________________________________

________________________________________________

### THOUGHTS

This is a great passage and one I relate to very easily. How about you? Sometimes I get depressed and angry saying, "Wow, Lord, sometimes it is hard being a Christian. I am sacrificing and giving up what I want to do with my time, sexuality, and money while trying to do what You want me to do. Is this going to pay off?" Now, most people would never be that honest with a pastor or God to say these things, but we all think them when times are tough. I find it very comforting that Peter asks a similar question that is unfiltered and very real!

After Jesus has talked to a rich man, He says that riches can sometimes get in the way of being God-focused. It is easier to lean on our money than to lean on God in prayer and trust. The Message Bible clarifies the wording and therefore the meaning. It basically asks if people are relying on themselves and therefore their money or if they are relying on God. When Jesus says this to the disciples, Peter is upset. He is worried about all of his effort and sacrifices to follow Jesus. He basically asks Him, "Jesus, we have given up a lot to follow You! Is this going to be worth it?"

Again, I love the Message Bible version of this, *"We left everything and followed you. What do we get out of it?"* It is just brilliantly visceral and honest!

Notice Jesus' response. Does He get angry? No. Does He have a meltdown and accuse them of being selfish? No. Does Jesus get moody and ignore them or quietly punish them by sulking? No! Does He get pompous like some pastors and leaders and lecture Peter on being "holy?" No! A Pharisee would have been incensed! The beauty of Jesus is that He is incredibly patient and He clearly instructs them. Jesus basically says, "Peter, it's all going to be worth it! Whatever you lose now, I will give you a hundred times as much in this life. And when My kingdom comes on the earth, you will all get new bodies, refreshed minds, and you will rule with Me forever on the earth! And I have some great rewards for you for overcoming evil and growing in goodness!" (my paraphrase).

One friend on a Zoom online study summarized Jesus' statement this way, "Peter, I will not forget your sacrifices! Be at peace. I will deeply reward you." His take was that Jesus was reassuring Peter!

When you step back for a moment from all the details and consider what Jesus is doing, it comes down to wonderful patience and clear rational instruction.

## TAKEAWAY

*"The glory of Christ, who is the image of God"* (2 Cor 4:4). This verse says that Jesus is the exact image of God. What did you see in the way Jesus relates to Peter, and what does it show you about God? Also, what does this imply for you, when you ask Jesus your deepest most visceral questions and desires? How will He respond to you? Use the line below and the Notes columns for your thoughts.

---

Jesus responds to Peter's question with mind-blowingly patient instruction. He is not exasperated! Instead He explains all the rewards in this life and of the coming kingdom. If Jesus is this way with Peter, that means God is responding to my concerns about the "cost" of following Jesus with the same patience and instruction. Jesus is the exact image of God. Glorious!

## NOTES

**Old Testament Link**

This reminds me of Jonah who was angry about all the comforts of home that he lost (his sacrifice) when God called him to preach to the Ninevites. That's why Jonah ran away. God patiently instructs Jonah with words and a plant. Jonah 4

NOTES

### FIRST COMMANDMENT PRAYER

Jesus, I love knowing You don't freak out and have a meltdown when Peter complains about his sacrifices. I love experiencing Your steadiness. You can handle it. You help Peter, and You build him up rather than tear him down! You're amazing! Seeing Your patience and goodness makes me want to follow You even more!

### WORSHIP WITHOUT MUSIC

How do Peter's worries about his sacrifice make you feel? Can you relate to him? What does it bring up for you? How do you think religious, Pharisee-type people could respond? Do you appreciate Jesus' response? Write two or three worship statements or use our starter lines:

________________________________________

________________________________________

Jesus, I love the way You______________________________

*Search Instagram and Facebook for God Is Just Like Jesus and say, "Hi."*

Take fifteen minutes out of your schedule and talk to Him about what delights and fascinates you about Him! Jot down on a scrap of paper your favorite three or four events from Days 1–6. See the "The Book" link on our website for starter worship statements to walk with. Or consider journaling to Him or meditating on Him, or dancing for Him, or creating art to Jesus. Express your wonder and delight in Jesus' goodness directly to Him!

## NOTES

Use this page as extra space for your notes and thoughts.

NOTES

# DAY 7 Discovery

## THE DISCIPLES RUN OFF THE CHILDREN

*People were bringing little children to Jesus for him to place his hands on them, but the disciples rebuked them. When Jesus saw this, he was indignant. He said to them, "Let the little children come to me, and do not hinder them, for the kingdom of God belongs to such as these. Truly I tell you, anyone who will not receive the kingdom of God like a little child will never enter it." And he took the children in his arms, placed his hands on them and blessed them. Mark 10:13-16*

*Then little children were brought to Him that He might put His hands on them and pray, but the disciples rebuked them. But Jesus said, "Let the little children come to Me, and do not forbid them; for of such is the kingdom of heaven." And He laid His hands on them and departed from there. Matt 19:13-15 (NKJV)*

*And He sat down, called the twelve, and said to them, "If anyone desires to be first, he shall be last of all and servant of all." Then He took a little child and set him in the midst of them. And when He had taken him in His arms, He said to them, "Whoever receives one of these little children in My name receives Me." Mark 9:35-37 (NKJV)*

*When I read slowly, I find things like Jesus' tenderness to take the child in His arms! I would have loved to have seen that!*

The first two passages describe the same event. The third passage describes a different event. Nevertheless, use them all. How does Jesus relate to the children? Is He aloof or engaged? What does He do? Is He distracted and busy or wonderfully present? How do you think the children felt being around Jesus? (Please use the Notes margins for extra space.)

____________________________________________________________

____________________________________________________________

How were the disciples failing here? How does Jesus react to the disciples? Why do you think the disciples were trying to send the children away?

____________________________________________________________

____________________________________________________________

Lastly, compare the two reactions you see in Jesus. Do you appreciate each one? Or not? Which one do you prefer? Why?

____________________________________________________________

____________________________________________________________

NOTES

THOUGHTS

These passages are packed full of insights into Jesus' character. Several different elements are revealed. First, let's focus on Jesus' tenderness and compassion toward the little children. Consider that Jesus is engaged in herculean tasks such as healing those who are diseased, delivering those oppressed by demons, training the disciples to lead the new church, confronting the majority of the Jewish religious leadership on hypocrisy, revealing the Father, and atoning for the sins of the human race! His goals were epic and staggering! In spite of that, He not only makes time for the children, but He greatly enjoys them! Jesus' tenderness for the children is revealed by the fact that He doesn't just pat them on the head or ask them a quick question. No, Jesus wants to spend some time with them and get His hands on them in love! The text says, *"he took the children in his arms,"* He likes these little guys and girls. He enjoys them. He takes time and holds them. He communicates His love and desire with a deep embrace!

You can see this again in Mark 9:36. Here Jesus is settling an argument between the disciples about which one of them is the greatest. Jesus teaches the disciples with a word picture involving one of the kids present:

> *He took a little child whom he placed among them. Taking the child in his arms, he said to them, "Whoever welcomes one of these little children in my name welcomes me." Mark 9:36*

The Message Bible puts it this way:

> *He put a child in the middle of the room. Then, cradling the little one in his arms, he said... Mark 9:36*

Jesus is doing something very important by conveying the great worth of this little child by affectionately taking him or her in His arms. He enjoys holding the child, smiling and talking with him or her. Jesus isn't just focused on executing the next task on His list like a corporate CEO or political leader. No! He is involved and present!

Thinking about Jesus really "liking" us as children and adults is a strange and wonderful thought! I usually just think about Him challenging me.

He is also doing more than mere intellectual teaching. He is trying to impress on His disciples, at a visceral heart level, how valuable these children are. This is not about structure, hierarchy, or pecking order. The kingdom of God is about people and relationships!

Secondly, let's consider another aspect of Jesus that is occurring right alongside His compassion. We don't know exactly why the disciples are trying to block the parents and children from being able to come to Jesus. Perhaps they thought Jesus was too busy? Maybe they thought the children were not important enough? Is this also an extension of the hierarchy mindset of "Who is the greatest?" The disciples are important, and adults are certainly more important than children, right? Regardless of the reasoning this is a bad place to be, between Jesus and the people He passionately loves! Jesus becomes indignant with the disciples! Let's define the word

**NOTES**

*I wonder if this is one of the reasons why Jesus gets so hot with the Pharisees when He drives out the money changers? The Pharisees were getting between Him and the people He loves!*

*He cares about us more than we know, and with a greater depth than we might desire sometimes, but it's all for our good.*

*indignant*. This is not a passive word. It has energy on it and some heat. Synonyms for indignant can include upset, irritated, hot, angry, incensed, mad, riled, or ticked off. When I think of Jesus, I think in terms of clean anger rather than what I would call *unclean anger*. Clean anger, in my mind, is using anger about a situation of injustice to accomplish some positive change without rejecting or beating anyone down. Unclean anger often involves being angry about one issue and then venting your anger on the next innocent person who walks by. Unclean anger accomplishes nothing positive. Unclean anger makes the situation even worse than it was.

In this event the disciples are trying to keep the little children from drawing near to Him, and Jesus is not pleased about this at all! You get insight into His passion for the children, and people generally, because He gets hot, incensed, or ticked off. Use whatever synonym you like, but Jesus is intense about this.

However, what does Jesus actually do? Jesus instructs and corrects His followers by commanding them not to block or hinder the little children from coming to Him! Now get this - He doesn't reject the disciples; instead He sees that it is time for correction so that they can change their actions and heart attitudes and become better shepherds. It is time to grow!

Now let's consider Jesus' complete lack of rejection. Does He tell Peter that he screwed up and to get lost? Does He kick James or John out of the inner leadership team? Does He quietly punish them with the silent treatment? No! No! No! Jesus brings correction without rejection. When you see there is no rejection in Jesus' actions, you can actually delight in His intensity to correct His followers. Why? Because His correction is good and it will protect and bless the community that is influenced and led by these leaders. The new church will need strong leaders, but they will also need safe, non-controlling leaders! The church needs healthy shepherds, not abusive leaders. Jesus' clean anger brings greater health to these new leaders!

When I was in high school, I had a coach who trained us to run cross country and track. I remember one track event where I was running as fast as I could to try to get under a five-minute mile. My coach was passionately yelling at me from the sidelines, "Come on, baby, you can do this!" I ran my heart out for him! I knew at that moment that all the running, the weight training, the pain, and the discipline was to make me stronger and faster! During my years of training, my coach wasn't trying to criticize me; he was challenging me to make me great! It was all for my good. It is the same thing with Jesus only more so. Jesus is the ultimate Coach! When you know your Coach cares about you like this, you can fully embrace the correction and discipline and grow from them rather than give up and quit! (This is the essence of Hebrews 12:5 on the next page.) Your personal growth can be greatly accelerated when you know your Coach has your absolute best in mind! Every word He speaks is for your good growth forever! This is a clear picture of Jesus' leadership in the lives of His followers. Jesus' correction and discipline can come with intensity and clean anger, but they are for our good and the good of the people around us.

However, because of our experiences in life, our own sinful choices and, lastly, our imperfect parents, we can misinterpret God's discipline and correction. I say more about how my own sinful choices affected my image of God in the Epilogue of this book. My own choices coupled with my dad's angry temperament made it really difficult for me to see Jesus correcting me without rejection. I had to see Jesus, time and time again, correcting the disciples in a wholesome way to even recognize it could be done differently than my dad did it. Year by year the Holy Spirit was reshaping my image of God to be more like the intense but good Coach!

I want to make a quick note about the word *discipline.* Discipline has such a negative connotation in our culture. I believe one of the reasons for this is because we are generally experiencing such a lack of emotional health in our culture. We have so few healthy role models. This is another reason for writing a book on Jesus' character. When emotionally unhealthy and broken people try to discipline their children, it often results in abusive behavior. However, we can have a healthy understanding of both correction and even discipline. Discipline is a consequence that is meant, not to tear us down, but to build us up. It is meant to teach us to abandon choices of selfishness, unclean anger, insecurity, or jealousy that would harm ourselves and harm others. Healthy discipline is meant to drive us to more emotionally healthy choices. A friend of mine named Andy said, "Discipline of children is never to be punitive (punishment) but should always be instructional." In other words, we should never punish our children for the mere sake of punishment. We should give thoughtful consequences so they can learn to avoid the problems and pain associated with lying, hurting other children, wounding others with words, and other such things. Therefore, correction and discipline should be thoughtful and completely meant to help people grow into greater goodness!

Read the passage below and use the margins to note the two negative responses to discipline you see in the Hebrews passage below. Also note the one very positive reason why the Lord disciplines us:

> *My son, do not make light of the Lord's discipline, and do not lose heart when he rebukes you, because the Lord disciplines the one he loves, and he chastens everyone he accepts as his son. Heb 12:5-6*

Did you write your answer in the notes column? It so important to get some thoughts down and really dig deep so you get the most from the Holy Spirit!

The writer of Hebrews warns us not to take the Lord's discipline too lightly and blow Him off. But the writer also tells us not to get overwhelmed by His discipline and quit. Avoid both of these responses. Because of my warped image of God, I would often get overwhelmed by God's correction and discipline rather than taking God lightly. Remember I said I had the mindset of the one-talent man from Matthew 25:24? I could totally lose heart and quit when He rebuked or corrected me. However, did you see God's positive motivation for His correction or discipline? What drives God is nothing less than deep love for you and me! God has no other desire except what is absolutely the best for you. He wants to grow us up in goodness, and that is going to bless us, bless all our relationships, family, children, friends, and even the strangers around us. That is called "good fruit."

Often we need to ask the Holy Spirit to bring clean understanding of who He is

## NOTES

*Jesus is the Lamb (compassion) and the Lion (clean anger).*

**Old Testament Link**

*The disciples' sin of running off the children and parents reminds me of Jonah running away from the Lord when he was called to preach repentance to Nineveh. Jesus disciples His followers, and God disciples Jonah with a storm and a whale until he repents. Jonah 1-2*

NOTES

during our failures and sins. Frequently we mistakenly feel that God is accusing and rejecting us (but that's the Devil's voice). Later we find out that the Master has not been relating that way to us at all. We have merely been transposing those character elements from the enemy onto God. The Holy Spirit can help us understand Jesus' work in our lives in a healthier way.

## TAKEAWAY

*"No one has ever seen God, but the one and only Son, who is himself God and is in closest relationship with the Father, has made him known"* (John 1:18). God is invisible, but Jesus has made Him known. What did you see in Jesus that revealed the Father to you? What does this mean for you when you are the vulnerable one coming to Jesus? Also, what does this mean for you when you're the one bossing someone else around?

---

Jesus' deep enjoyment and compassion for the children reveals the Father's enjoyment and compassion for them and for us! Jesus' correction of the disciples without rejecting them reveals how the Father may challenge and correct us but without rejection. His correction or discipline may come to us with intensity but never with accusation, rejection, or shame. His correction is always for our own good to make us greater and better able to care about others, in order that we would become quality human beings!

## FIRST COMMANDMENT PRAYER

Jesus, I love seeing Your compassion and tenderness with the little children. You enjoy the children and delight in them, and You delight in us. You also strongly correct the disciples for treating the children as less important or valuable. I love Your discipline of Your followers that has no rejection in it. You challenge them for their good. And if that is what You are like, then I can handle Your correction and embrace it and grow from it! You are awesome! I want to be just like You, Jesus!

## WORSHIP WITHOUT MUSIC

Often, talking "about" Jesus is easy and feels fine. However, talking "to" Jesus can sometimes feel uncomfortable, almost too intimate. Push through any uncomfortable and awkward feelings and write two or three worship statements directly to Jesus about things in this passage that stir your heart. Use the "starter" lines below or scratch them out and invent your own!

Jesus, the way You ______________________________ is

wonderful!

Jesus, I'm delighted by Your______________________________________

Jesus, Your__________________________________________ is awesome!

Invent your own worship:

________________________________________________

________________________________________________

**NOTES**

*Consider listening to the series on audio podcasts. Search for "God Is Just Like Jesus" on Apple Podcasts, Spotify, or Amazon Music apps.*

NOTES

# DAY 8 Discovery

## THOMAS DOUBTS THAT JESUS IS ALIVE

*Now Thomas (also known as Didymus), one of the Twelve, was not with the disciples when Jesus came. So the other disciples told him, "We have seen the Lord!" But he said to them, "Unless I see the nail marks in his hands and put my finger where the nails were, and put my hand into his side, I will not believe." A week later his disciples were in the house again, and Thomas was with them. Though the doors were locked, Jesus came and stood among them and said, "Peace be with you!" Then he said to Thomas, "Put your finger here; see my hands. Reach out your hand and put it into my side. Stop doubting and believe." Thomas said to him, "My Lord and my God!" Then Jesus told him, "Because you have seen me, you have believed; blessed are those who have not seen and yet have believed." John 20:24-29*

*When they came back from the tomb, they told all these things to the Eleven and to all the others. It was Mary Magdalene, Joanna, Mary the mother of James, and the others with them who told this to the apostles. But they did not believe the women, because their words seemed to them like nonsense. Peter, however, got up and ran to the tomb. Bending over, he saw the strips of linen lying by themselves, and he went away, wondering to himself what had happened. Luke 24:9-12*

*It's good to know that Thomas and the other ten disciples (a.k.a. the Apostles) struggled with doubts and unbelief like I do.*

*While they were still talking about this, Jesus himself stood among them and said to them, "Peace be with you." They were startled and frightened, thinking they saw a ghost. He said to them, "Why are you troubled, and why do doubts rise in your minds? Look at my hands and my feet. It is I myself! Touch me and see; a ghost does not have flesh and bones, as you see I have." When he had said this, he showed them his hands and feet. And while they still did not believe it because of joy and amazement, he asked them, "Do you have anything here to eat?" They gave him a piece of broiled fish, and he took it and ate it in their presence. He said to them, "This is what I told you while I was still with you: Everything must be fulfilled that is written about me in the Law of Moses, the Prophets and the Psalms." Then he opened their minds so they could understand the Scriptures Luke 24:36-45*

Think of a few ways the Devil would have related to Thomas's disbelief if he were in Jesus' position. Write out some statements that might reflect his unhealthy motivation methods:

______________________________________________

______________________________________________

Now contrast Jesus with the Devil or a Pharisee, and take a minute and write down the attitude Jesus had toward Thomas's failure to believe. This is critical for you to do honestly. How did Jesus interact with Thomas? From your gut, how do you think

NOTES

Jesus felt toward Thomas?

______________________________________________

______________________________________________

THOUGHTS

Let's think for a minute about this event with Thomas. The women have seen Jesus, and they told the disciples. However, some time has passed because the excitement has died down and Cleopas and the other disciples found the time to walk out of Jerusalem down the road to Emmaus and meet Jesus. I explore this passage from Luke 24 in one of the Additional Study Passages. These two return and tell the disciples that they saw Jesus, but Thomas is not with the other ten disciples. Thomas is adamant that if he doesn't see Jesus, put his finger into the nail holes in Jesus' hands, and put his finger into the spear hole in Jesus' side, then he will not believe that Jesus came back from the dead. A week later, Jesus shows up among the disciples once again. How does Jesus approach Thomas?

By writing down the answer to those questions above, you can get a clearer picture of how you see Jesus. It gives you clues about your image of God. You have to know "where you are" to know "where you need to go" in terms of having a healthier image of God. My friend Brian Krueger says, "Isn't it interesting that Jesus doesn't lead with accusation or shame?" A Pharisee or a very critical person might say, "I told you I would rise from the dead! Was it really so hard to believe the other ten disciples?" How about the typical, "I told you so?" Or how about, "For crying out loud, you guys are about to lead the entire church! Didn't I tell you I would rise from the dead? How am I supposed to save the world with you guys as my top leaders?"

However, Jesus doesn't do that.

What I am trying to say here is that Jesus does not motivate His followers with accusation, guilt, condemnation, or shame! That is huge for us to realize because in life we can fall into the enemy's way of motivating people. And we don't even realize it!

*Jesus is steadier and more patient with our fears and sins than I realized.*

Jesus shows up and basically instructs Thomas, "Put your finger here." Jesus then challenges him, possibly with a tone of correction or discipline, "Stop doubting and believe." Be very careful to notice that, once again, Jesus doesn't reject Thomas for his sin of unbelief, nor does He heap on the condemnation. Jesus doesn't remove Thomas from being one of His twelve disciples. Additionally, Jesus doesn't reject Thomas personally. And remember, Thomas also denied Jesus along with the other disciples. After all these failures and sins, Jesus still embraces Thomas, and He challenges and corrects Thomas to make him greater and grow his faith. It is Jesus' love for Thomas that is the motivation for His instruction, challenge, and even correction.

I think it is also important to realize that Thomas wasn't the only one sinning in unbelief. All of the disciples failed to believe the women who had seen Jesus! They all

## NOTES

*Old Testament Link*

*Thomas's doubting that Jesus is alive reminds me of Abraham doubting that God will protect him. Abraham sins and lies to Abimelech saying Sarah, his wife, was only his sister. Jesus instructs and corrects Thomas, and God corrects Abraham through Abimelech and his dream. Genesis 20*

failed to remember that Jesus said He would be killed and come back to life. My guess is that Jesus talked figuratively so often that they didn't think He was really going to die or really come back to life. Remember He said to Nicodemus, *"Unless you are born again"* (John 3:3) or *"Be on your guard against the yeast of the Pharisees and Sadducees"* (Matt 16:5). *"Unless you eat the flesh of the Son of Man and drink His blood, you have no life in you"* (John 6:53). Anyway, it is just a guess, but it might be worth thinking about.

And what does He do? He instructs them. He doesn't accuse them of unbelief, or condemn them or reject them. He instructs them to touch His hands and feet. And when they still can't believe it for joy, He asks them if they have any physical food, like fish. And then He instructs them in a physical event, much like calling the fish into Peter's net or washing their feet; He actually eats the fish right in front of them, even though He has been dead! I call it *visceral instruction*. It's an experience with Jesus that is more than just a mental exercise! But that is what He does with them, instruction not fault-finding.

Lastly, Jesus challenges Thomas, and us, to press on in faith saying, *"blessed are those who have not seen and yet have believed."* Jesus is always calling us higher in goodness and faith. But remember our obedience to Him does not earn acceptance with Him. We are already accepted through the cross! But doing what He says brings more protection and prosperity into our lives and those around us. However, His reason for challenging and correcting us is so that we might bear more good fruit in this broken world and love those around us!

### TAKEAWAY

*"...the gospel that displays the glory of Christ, who is the image of God"* (2 Cor 4:4). Jesus is the image of God! Wow! What did you see in Jesus as He interacts with Thomas's unbelief that shows you something good about God? What about your own doubt and unbelief? What is the significance for you?

____________________________________________

____________________________________________

The fact that Jesus instructs and challenges Thomas without shaming him reveals that God instructs and challenges us without shaming us. He is the Good Shepherd! Jesus perfectly reveals the Father.

**NOTES**

## FIRST COMMANDMENT PRAYER

Jesus, You are wonderful! Once again You don't lead with accusation relative to Thomas's unbelief. I love how You instruct and challenge him to become great! You are not passive toward our failures; You care but in a healthy way! You call us higher in goodness for our good and those around us! I delight in You!

### WORSHIP WITHOUT MUSIC

Can you relate to Thomas? I sure can! Even after all he has seen and experienced for three and a half years, he's still struggling to believe in Jesus during the next crisis. It's crazy how the next real threat or fear can cause me to wrestle with unbelief. But Jesus is willing to instruct and correct me, and you, to help us grow, just like Thomas.

Tell Jesus what you love about how He relates to Thomas and us in our unbelief. He doesn't want to push us away after failure but pull us close! Tell Him how you feel about His instruction and correction without rejection that is designed to cause us to grow in goodness!

___

___

*Online Zoom discussions with a small group of people are the single best way to process and digest Jesus' good character and experience your image of God shifting for the better. Look for "Online Discussions" on our website.*

NOTES

I guess they were hacked off on Jesus' behalf? Seems a little intense wanting to kill everyone?

# DAY 9 Discovery

## JAMES AND JOHN WANT TO WIPE OUT THE SAMARITAN VILLAGE

*As the time approached for him to be taken up to heaven, Jesus resolutely set out for Jerusalem. And he sent messengers on ahead, who went into a Samaritan village to get things ready for him; but the people there did not welcome him, because he was heading for Jerusalem. When the disciples James and John saw this, they asked, "Lord, do you want us to call fire down from heaven to destroy them, just as Elijah did?" But Jesus turned and rebuked them. And He said, "You do not know what kind of spirit you are of, for the Son of Man did not come to destroy men's lives, but to save them." And he and his disciples went to another village. Luke 9:51-56 (Footnotes for verses 54-56 included)*

Why are James and John so angry? What do they want to do to the Samaritans? How does Jesus respond to James and John? Lastly, how does Jesus act toward the Samaritans?

________________________________________________________

________________________________________________________

### THOUGHTS

It is near the end of Jesus' three and a half years of ministry. Jesus commits Himself to go to Jerusalem to suffer and die for the sins of the human race. The Message Bible says, *"he gathered up his courage and steeled himself for the journey to Jerusalem"* (Luke 9:51). As He is walking through Israel toward Jerusalem, He sends messengers ahead of them to a Samaritan village. Jesus wants to stay there overnight. The Samaritans, however, reject Jesus' request because He is heading for Jerusalem and there are religious tensions between the Samaritans and Jews. James and John see the Samaritan rejection of Jesus' request for food and lodging and are offended and furious! They ask Jesus if they can call down fire or a lightning strike on the Samaritans to kill them. They must be thinking of what Elijah did to the false prophets of Baal (1 Kings 18). There is a footnote on Luke 9:54, some manuscripts add on the words "even as Elijah did" to James and John's statement. James and John are confusing ordinary, immature people with the hardened, rebellious, demon-worshiping priests of Baal. (Remember, those who worshiped Baal or Ashtoreth would cause some of their children to be sacrificed in the fire. See 2 Chr 28:3, 33:6; Jer 7:31, 19:2–6. Those who worshiped these so-called gods engaged in the most horrific practices to the modern mind.) To say the least, James and John are furious with the Samaritan village.

It is also really important to realize that Elijah didn't pray for a lightning bolt to destroy the people but to consume the sacrifice. James and John are really distorting this event in their unhealthy anger. In numerous ways it is the complete opposite of what Jesus has preached in the Sermon on the Mount! (They must not have been listening.)

Let's pause for a moment and ask ourselves, "How did Jesus, Himself, respond to the Samaritans' rejection? Does He get angry like the two brothers? Does He get hurt and offended like one of us might? Think of a world leader who gets snubbed or slighted by a leader of a city or a region. Wonderfully, Jesus does none of those things. He demonstrates incredible humility considering His limitless power over human sickness, over the demonic and angelic realms, and over nature itself. Jesus merely turns away from the Samaritan village, looks down the road, and tired as He was, begins walking to the next village. The text says, *"And he and his disciples went to another village."* The God-Man merely walks on down the road with no anger, no threats, and no insecurity. Radically humble! It is a great example of Jesus turning the other cheek. It's just another reason to delight in Him and worship Him!

Now let's turn to consider how Jesus responds to James and John themselves. The text says, *"Jesus turned and rebuked them."* The NIV Bible footnote says that Jesus rebuked James and John saying, *"You do not know what kind of spirit you are of, for the Son of Man did not come to destroy men's lives but to save them."*

We know that James and John are offended at the Samaritans and their anger is so intense they want to kill the whole village. This isn't just a screw-up; this is nothing less than outright, grievous sin. This is sinful unhealthy anger. Jesus turns to James and John and rebukes them!

Rebuke isn't a word we use in our language, so let's define it. The dictionary defines rebuke as "an expression of sharp disapproval." Some synonyms include reprove, reprimand, upbraid, and reproach. This isn't a passive or sissy word. Jesus is sharply correcting His followers! There is intensity, and there is vigor in His actions! Jesus isn't just being calm. He is intensely correcting His well-meaning but very misdirected disciples!

Jesus' healthy anger with his followers is raw discipline, but without rejection. Jesus is sharply training His future leaders to be self-controlled and wise instead of engaging in rash anger. To want to destroy an entire group of people merely over an offense is evil. The soon-to-be apostles need this severe discipline to change and become leaders that are safe to govern the flock instead of becoming angry abusers. This is really good!

Often we are afraid of correction or discipline. However, most of this stems from a fear of being rejected either personally or positionally. As we review Jesus' correction, we find the Gardener is pruning us for one reason: good growth (John 15:2). As the fear of rejection is removed, we can give ourselves to Jesus' discipline (pruning) and rejoice in growth even though it might involve pain. As stated previously, another way to see Jesus is as the good Coach who can discipline His athletes so that they can be the absolute best players and team-leaders that they can be!

Let's look at how Jesus motivates the disciples compared to how the Devil would

**NOTES**

*Jesus' healthy anger toward His leaders and His protection for the Samaritans go hand in hand, two sides of one coin.*

*Jesus' patience with the Samaritans is a great example of 1 Peter 3:9, "He is patient with you, not wanting any to perish, but everyone to come to repentance."*

**NOTES**

do it. The Devil would swoop in with the typical accusation, condemnation, shame, and rejection. The Devil or a Pharisee would start with accusation: "Man, are you guys idiots! They are just people, not the demon worshiping priests of Baal! Don't you guys know anything?" After this, shame is usually employed: "Honestly, I don't know if you guys will ever figure this out. I spend all this time with you, and you keep sinning and wanting to hurt people. You'll never measure up." How about the Devil's favorite, rejection: "There has to be better disciples somewhere that I can find to do a good job instead of you losers!"

Now let's refocus on Jesus' healthy motivation. When you are relating to God, His goal is to help you change and repent. When we are parenting, we need to remember the goal is not to make our children feel bad over a mistake or sin, but to help them change and grow. As I said previously but it bears repeating, "Godly discipline is always instructional; it should not be punitive." Good discipline is always a consequence meant to instruct us in goodness and not merely punish. Again, the goal is growth, not feeling bad. Just feeling bad isn't going to get you anywhere. It just results in more dysfunctional thinking and unhealthy emotional patterns. This is part of what Paul calls "the flesh."

*Old Testament Link*
*James and John's bitter response and desire to kill the Samaritans reminds me of David's bitter response and desire to kill Nabal and his entire household. God stops David through Abigail's instruction even as Jesus rebukes the disciples and instructs them.*
*1 Samuel 25 (Nabal's offense, v. 10; David's fury, v. 21; Abigail's instruction v. 23-31.)*

Jesus' motivation to rebuke the disciples is so that they will not harm regular, everyday people. This is why I love the footnote so much. Jesus doesn't say the things the Devil or a Pharisee would. Jesus, in the rebuke, reminds the disciples of their identity in the Holy Spirit and their mission to save people, not to destroy them. *"You do not know what kind of spirit you are of, for the Son of Man did not come to destroy men's lives, but to save them"* (Luke 9:55-56 footnote). Jesus' healthy motivation is so different from the way some human bosses motivate their leaders. Jesus knows how to rebuke and also how to build up the disciples to be healthy leaders! He is the ultimate Coach!

Lastly, it is important to know what Jesus gets angry about and what He does not get angry about. Jesus gets angry when the disciples try to drive the little children away or when the Pharisees take over the temple and oppress the everyday people who are trying to come to God. However, Jesus does not get angry about the Samaritans rejecting Him because He is a Jew and going to Jerusalem. He just moves on. Jesus differentiates between healthy and unhealthy anger.

### TAKEAWAY

*"He is the image of the invisible God"* (Col 1:15). Since Jesus is the image of the invisible God, what did He reveal to you about God as He responded to James and John's aggression? What is the significance of this when you suggest something really crazy because you are offended? How does He respond to you?

---

Jesus' discipline of James and John has no condemnation, shame, or rejection in it. He is disciplining them for their own good. This reveals the way the Father disciplines us when we are seriously engaged in sin. He intensely corrects us for our own good and the good of those we will influence. His healthy discipline results in protection for all! Additionally, Jesus' humility to overlook the Samaritan insult reveals God's humility to overlook insults. He's pretty radical!

## FIRST COMMANDMENT PRAYER

Jesus I love that You're not passive and You don't ignore the disciples aggression! I love that You bring correction to Your followers so that they would be less dangerous and might grow to be better leaders. Thank You that You are not passive in these situations, but You are strong and intense because You care about people! I also love the fact that You are not angry with the Samaritans but You turn and humbly walk away! Your power is unlimited, but Your humility is central to Your radically unique personality! I delight in Your goodness! But I also want to be more like You! Draw me to You and help me be just like You!

## WORSHIP WITHOUT MUSIC

Do you relate to James and John? Have you ever been so offended that you had horrible, violent thoughts toward others? If we are truly honest, that's probably all of us at one time or another.

Journal or talk to Jesus about what you appreciate about His response to James and John, or to the Samaritans.

Jesus, I'm grateful for Your response to James and John because....

________________________________________________

________________________________________________

Go on a fifteen-minute prayer walk and tell Him what His response to them, and to yourself, means to you. Take your favorite three to five worship declarations written on 3 x 5 cards and tell Him how amazing He is!

Even simple worship statements to Him increase your capacity to worship. Don't let pride or awkwardness stop you from adoring the One who laid His life down for you!

**NOTES**

*Have you seen the YouTube videos on this series? Search YouTube for "God Is Just Like Jesus." Enjoy.*

NOTES

I love the fact that the two men (Moses and Elijah) who meet with Jesus here had epic failures and sins in their lives in the middle of other victories! God is not the God of those who are perfect (there are no such people), but He is the God of those who will respond to Him!

# DAY 10 Discovery

## PETER DRAWS ATTENTION TO HIMSELF DURING A HOLY MOMENT

*About eight days after Jesus said this, he took Peter, John and James with him and went up onto a mountain to pray. As he was praying, the appearance of his face changed, and his clothes became as bright as a flash of lightning. Two men, Moses and Elijah, appeared in glorious splendor, talking with Jesus. They spoke about his departure, which he was about to bring to fulfillment at Jerusalem. Peter and his companions were very sleepy, but when they became fully awake, they saw his glory and the two men standing with him. As the men were leaving Jesus, Peter said to him, "Master, it is good for us to be here. Let us put up three shelters–one for you, one for Moses and one for Elijah." (He did not know what he was saying.) While he was speaking, a cloud appeared and covered them, and they were afraid as they entered the cloud. A voice came from the cloud, saying, "This is my Son, whom I have chosen; listen to him." When the voice had spoken, they found that Jesus was alone. The disciples kept this to themselves and did not tell anyone at that time what they had seen. Luke 9:28-36*

*They turned out to be Moses and Elijah–and what a glorious appearance they made! They talked over his exodus, the one Jesus was about to complete in Jerusalem. Luke 9:31 (MSG)*

*When the disciples heard this, they fell facedown to the ground, terrified. But Jesus came and touched them. "Get up," he said. "Don't be afraid." When they looked up, they saw no one except Jesus. Matt 17:6-8*

Describe what is happening here in your own words. How would you have reacted if you had been Peter, James, or John? Why do you think Peter is talking? Where is the attention and focus before Peter starts talking, and where is it after? How do you feel about the Father's response? Put Jesus' response into your own words.

____________________________________________

____________________________________________

### THOUGHTS

Jesus takes Peter, James, and John up a high mountain and is transfigured before them. The Shekinah Glory that only appeared over the Mercy Seat on the Ark of the Covenant in the Old Testament covers Jesus, emanating from His body! His human disguise is momentarily put aside, revealing that He is more than human while He talks with Moses and Elijah about His "departure" or death on the cross (Luke 9:31). The Message interestingly uses the word *exodus* hinting at the deeper significance of their discussion. In an abrupt manner, Peter erupts into babbling in the middle of this sacred supernatural moment. He assures Jesus that, *"It is good that we are here!"* (Face palm!) Peter informs these three that he could do some significant things for them, like constructing three memorials or shelters for them to rest or dwell in! It would be absolutely comical if the moment wasn't so supernatural and "other-worldly"!

It is difficult to know WHY Peter is speaking! No one is speaking to him. It is fascinating that he didn't merely watch and learn during such an overwhelming event! Regardless, what occurs is amazing. The Father Himself does what we have seen Jesus do time and time again. *"While he was still speaking, a bright cloud covered them, and a voice from the cloud said, 'This is my Son, whom I love; with him I am well pleased. Listen to him!' When the disciples heard this, they fell facedown to the ground, terrified"* (Matt 17:5). The Father Himself is patient with Peter's foolishness and actually instructs him. "Peter, close your mouth and keep your eyes on Jesus" (my paraphrase). To be sure, it is a very intense encounter with the Father Himself! However, when you look at the experience, it is essentially instruction mixed with some challenge and correction. It's continually important to disassociate intensity from rejection. Neither the Father nor Jesus are rejecting Peter. Both are reorienting Peter to align with them. Just because something is intense does not mean it is bad. Intensity can be required to drive an experience or lesson deep within our hearts. It can be very good.

Additionally, the Father may be taking Peter's, James', and John's eyes off Moses and Elijah and setting them firmly back on Jesus. Let's not be distracted by glory or angels, but let's set our eyes firmly on Jesus!

Imagine yourself somehow being present in a conversation between Billy Graham, Bill Johnson, and a secret leader of the Chinese underground church. They are discussing events so profound that you struggle to even understand the issues. Then, for some reason, you blunder in with some completely random idea and break the flow of the entire conversation, inadvertently putting all the focus on yourself! That is exactly what Peter did.

I don't know that this is "sin" or just a huge "screw up" – but it clearly reveals the patience and instruction of both Jesus and, even, the Father! (Remember, the Father is the One who sits on the Throne from Revelation 4 and 5 and Daniel 7:9-10.)

How do you think typical people would respond if they were Jesus or the Father? How would you have responded if you were processing something so critical, and someone that you permit to listen and learn blurts out completely unrelated thoughts and content?

---

When Peter, James, and John dare to open their eyes, they only see Jesus. Notice that Jesus doesn't find fault with Peter or tell him he screwed up the entire holy moment. There is no accusation of sin or failure. Jesus is patient, and He actually encourages Peter. Remember the text says they were "terrified" or "scared to death" (is how the Message words it) after God speaks. The text tenderly says Jesus "touched them."

**NOTES**

**Old Testament Link**
Peter's breaking this holy moment reminds me of Moses being called by God in the Burning Bush. Moses ignores the epic moment and asks the Lord if He can't get someone else to do the job. God instructs Peter, and God instructs Moses.
Exodus 3-4

NOTES

Then He says, "Get up," and "Don't be afraid" (Matt 17:7). It's delightful really, given the intensity of the situation!

Take some time to research Moses' and Elijah's lives since these are the two that are honored enough to get to show up and process Jesus' crucifixion with Him. Moses has great failures (that may be hard to understand) that I reference in the Notes column. Elijah also has a great failure that I reference in the Day 10 Notes column. Given my old mindset regarding who God was, I used to fear that He rejected Moses or Elijah for their failures. I couldn't understand correction without rejection. One day I was delighted to realize that both Moses and Elijah were the ones to show up here and process Jesus' death and, probably, resurrection with Him. It really warmed my heart!

### TAKEAWAY

*"When he looks at me [Jesus], he sees the one who sent me"* (John 12:45). This one is reversed! Here we see the Father and find out that it confirms what we have seen in Jesus so often. What did you see in the Father that confirmed things you have seen in Jesus? Also write about what this means for you when you are the one drawing attention to yourself or being confused about what to do or say in a particular situation.

---

Here we see a unique event where the Father Himself demonstrates the same character that we see in Jesus. There is instruction and correction without rejection, and He doesn't shame the disciples. God is just like Jesus, and Jesus is just like God. They are one and the same!

### FIRST COMMANDMENT PRAYER

Father, I delight in Your patience and instruction! Whether it is sin or just a screw-up, I know You won't reject me but will work with me in patience to "grow me up"! That gives me confidence to "go for it" in faith and serve You with my whole heart! I want to be just like You. Help me be patient with my family, friends, and people I work with! You're amazing!

### WORSHIP WITHOUT MUSIC

Have you ever unintentionally or intentionally drawn all the attention onto yourself in a personal moment between other people? Write the event down. How did people react to you? How is Jesus' response different than other people's responses?

What do you like about the Father and Jesus from this passage? Put it in your own words, speak to Him, and tell Him directly.

Father, I love how You ______________________________________________

Jesus, Your ______________________________________________ is awesome.

Put your favorite three to five responses to Jesus on a scrap of paper, a 3 x 5 card, or on your phone. Then go out on a fifteen-to thirty-minute prayer walk and talk directly to Jesus about what fascinates you about Him, about what delights you about Him, about what you like or love about Him! Feed on His goodness and train yourself to eat at His table and nourish yourself on Him alone!

**NOTES**

*If you want more information on the Old Testament Links, see "The Book" on our website and look for O.T. Link Information. www.GodIsJustLikeJesus.com*

NOTES

It's interesting there were other boats with the boat that held the disciples.

# DAY 11 Discovery

## THE DISCIPLES ARE AFRAID OF THE FURIOUS STORM

*That day when evening came, he said to his disciples, "Let us go over to the other side." Leaving the crowd behind, they took him along, just as he was, in the boat. There were also other boats with him. A furious squall came up, and the waves broke over the boat, so that it was nearly swamped. Jesus was in the stern, sleeping on a cushion. The disciples woke him and said to him, "Teacher, don't you care if we drown?" He got up, rebuked the wind and said to the waves, "Quiet! Be still!" Then the wind died down and it was completely calm. He said to his disciples, "Why are you so afraid? Do you still have no faith?" They were terrified and asked each other, "Who is this? Even the wind and the waves obey him!" Mark 4:35-41 (Consider reviewing the parallel passages of this event in Matt 8:23-27 and Luke 8:22-25)*

*"Teacher, is it nothing to you that we're going to drown?" Mark 4:38 (MSG)*

*They were in absolute awe, staggered. "Who is this anyway?" they asked. "Wind and sea at his beck and call!" Mark 4:41 (MSG)*

How would you portray the situation, the disciples' fears, and especially Jesus' response to the disciples' fears? How do you interpret what Jesus is saying to them?

______________________________________________

______________________________________________

### THOUGHTS

Some churches and people represent Jesus as only meek and mild. Here, though, is a situation where He is definitely fierce and intense. It's so important that we do not polarize Jesus into only one side or the other. We need the Holy Spirit to show us how meekness and fierceness mix in perfect goodness in Jesus, so we can understand how these seemingly opposite characteristics combine perfectly in God. Jesus is both the Lion and the Lamb!

Jesus decides to go over to the other side of Lake Galilee (Mark 4:35). He leaves the crowd and gets into the boat. There were other boats with them. As they cross the Sea of Galilee, a furious storm arises and begins pounding the boats with waves and filling them with water. In the midst of the terrible storm, their boats begin to sink. The threat of drowning is very real, so real in fact that seasoned fishermen were terrified! However, the disciples find Jesus sleeping in the stern; they wake Him exclaiming, *"Teacher, don't you care if we drown?"* I love the Message version as well, *"Teacher, is it nothing to you that we're going to drown?"* There is a root fear and insecurity here. Part of what they are expressing is, "Do You even care about us?" Jesus answers that insecurity with a resounding, "Yes," as He crushes the threatening storm! There is an unspoken command in there to them and us not to misinterpret

His deep concern for us when life's circumstances are dire and we are despairing. Be assured, the Lord still cares for each of us! So, there is something here in Jesus' character about reassurance.

So let's talk about the disciples' fear. Please know that I'm not trying to be critical here. If I was in their situation, I would probably fare far worse. So, with that said, we have to look at their response to the storm. Even though they have seen the sick healed, those demonically oppressed set free, and the water turned to wine, they are completely overwhelmed by the storm, and their confidence in Jesus totally fails. Sometimes it is one thing to see someone else struggle and then God help them. We say, "Why don't they just trust God?" But it can be another thing when we are the one in the middle of the storm and we have to trust God. Then we say, "God, where are You?" Do you relate to this? I sure do, especially during really stressful or painful times in my life! Was this the first miracle that was directly centered around Jesus saving them? Possibly. Regardless, their faith in Jesus completely collapses, and sometimes ours does too. If you read the life of King David, you will see that this happens a number of times when He is running from Saul.

How does Jesus respond? Jesus gets up, instantly assesses the situation, and immediately takes control, silencing the wind, the waves, and the furious storm. "Quiet! Be Still!" (Notice the exclamation marks! He's intense!) Then the wind dies down, and everything becomes completely calm.

One of the things I like about Jesus, even in the middle of His intense response, is His raw protection of the disciples! The more I process this event, the more I can savor and enjoy that aspect of Him!

Next, Jesus turns to his disciples saying, *"Why are you so afraid? Do you still have no faith?"* Luke 8:25 says, *"Where is your faith?"* Matthew 8:26 says, *"You of little faith... why are you so afraid?"*

What do you hear in Jesus' words? How do you interpret them? Use the line and the Notes column.

---

Here we must wrestle with Jesus' words, *"Why are you so afraid? Do you still have no faith?"* Again, if you can get the fault-finding, accusation, and rejection out of your image of God, then you can look at this passage in a healthier way.

In years past I just read Jesus' response with a deep sense of Him being frustrated, angry, and accusing the disciples of failure. I know, my bad image of God just coming to the surface again : ) However, I also began to see there was instruction here. As I said before, if we can disconnect intensity from rejection, we can connect the dots and realize that Jesus is not rejecting them here but is doing some very intense, heavy-duty instruction and training of the disciples! Since He is not rejecting them, He is after something, right? What could that be? Someone on a Zoom online

## NOTES

**Old Testament Link**

The disciples' faith failing reminds me of Elijah's faith failing when Jezebel threatens his life after he killed the 450 demon-prophets of Baal. The disciples say, "Lord, don't you care that we will drown?" Elijah says, "I have had enough, Lord... Take my life." God/Jesus brings Elijah a supernatural meal and instructs and corrects Elijah in a cave at Horeb by demonstrating that God's power is much greater than Jezebel's. 1 Kings 19:1-18

NOTES

meeting said, "Maybe Jesus is training them for their leadership of the new church and martyrdom?" Jesus knows they will have confrontations with the same Pharisees that would kill Him. He also knows that they will have conflicts with King Herod and Rome. Remember, James get killed in Acts 12:2. So maybe, as intense as this is, the experience is a lot more about preparation and training than any sense of fault-finding and rejection. It reminds me of Jesus talking to Peter after he sank on the water and saying, "Keep your eyes on Me! Don't be distracted by fear. You can do this" (my paraphrase).

Ok, so there is intense instruction. You could probably also read in some correction or even discipline. Given all they have already experienced being around Jesus, He may have really been rebuking their fear that was completely out of control. But again, even if Jesus is getting that intense with them, He is doing it, not to tear them down, but to build them up. He is calling them higher in faith for their good and the good of the people they will pastor. He really loves them and wants them to become all that they can be as His beloved sons and daughters!

Jesus may be saying something along the lines of, "Why are you so afraid? You are with Me! Your confidence in Me can grow! So let it grow! I can handle this and absolutely anything else that occurs!" (my paraphrase). He is challenging Peter and all of them to grow and trust Him more, regardless of the threat.

Just to reiterate it one more time, we have to realize that Jesus is not rejecting Peter or the disciples for being fearful and failing to trust Him. Jesus doesn't demote Peter in leadership or in personal relationship. Remember, Jesus doesn't reject Peter for huge failures like denying Him publicly before the servant girl (John 18:15-18). Therefore, since Jesus doesn't reject Peter for the big things, Jesus isn't rejecting Peter for smaller things. We need to see that Jesus works day and night to build up Peter through encouragement, instruction, challenge, correction, and even discipline! Jesus is the Master at building people up! As Ephesians 2:10 says, *"We are His workmanship."*

Lastly, this entire experience is really a worship opportunity! It's another experience where Jesus reveals His hidden identity much like what happened on the Mount of Transfiguration or Jesus walking on water or Jesus washing their feet. Awe and amazement consume the disciples! This experience of His deliverance in the storm impacts the disciples at a visceral level and changes them. The text clearly highlights that it creates worship in their hearts. The Message Bible says it so profoundly, *"They were in absolute awe, staggered. 'Who is this any way?' they asked. 'Wind and sea at his beck and call!'"* They are experiencing hair-raising revelation that Jesus is more than a mere teacher, a healer, or even a prophet. Not even Elijah spoke to the air and commanded it to rain. Elijah had to pray and ask God to make it rain (1 King 18). Jesus speaks directly to nature, and it obeys His command! This is one of dozens of ways that He reveals His divinity. He reveals His veiled identity to all who will look and listen. Their response (and ours) is raw worship! In the end this is how God reveals Himself to Job in the storm in chapter Job 38:1 and 42:1-6. The Message says it so beautifully, *"I admit I once lived by rumors of you; now I have it all firsthand–from my own eyes and ears!"* Job encounters God from chapter 38–42, and it left him in utter

NOTES

awe, worshiping God because God is both powerful and absolutely good! Job drops all of his complaints and criticism of God in the depths of worship!

### TAKEAWAY

*"The Son is the radiance of God's glory and the exact representation of his being"* (Heb 1:3). In this intense event, what did Jesus show you about the Father? Have you had to wrestle with Jesus' intensity from Bible passages or events in your own life? What did you learn here that can help you process His intensity in a good way?

---

Jesus' intensity, without rejection, is meant to train and prepare the disciples to lead the new church and reveals God's intensity, without rejection, for them! It is also meant to train and prepare us for life. *"In all things God works for the good of those who love Him, who have been called according to His purpose"* (Rom 8:28).

### FIRST COMMANDMENT PRAYER

Father, I love seeing that You are not accusing the disciples, but You are intensely challenging them to grow so they can maintain their focus on You as they face life-threatening events in the future! It is wonderful to see Your intensity has a good and clear purpose! Thank You for helping us grow, even if it hurts sometimes. As humans we hate struggling, to say nothing of suffering. However, help us know the importance of struggling as we grow like the caterpillar into the butterfly and fly in faith! You can't remove the struggle without removing the strength it creates! The more we know You are in charge, the more we know You will redeem and use every struggle! Help us, like Jacob, wrestle with You and come out with a new name and new strength! You are the ultimate Coach!

### WORSHIP WITHOUT MUSIC

When you read a passage about Jesus intensely challenging or correcting His followers, what comes up in your heart? How do you feel? Do you feel yourself pulling back from Him or leaning into Him?

Can you connect with the fact that Jesus doesn't accuse them or reject them for their failure?

Can you internalize that His intensity and challenge come out of His love for them to grow in goodness and strength? Also connect with the fact that during this event they all get a revelation that Jesus is more than a mere human teacher, healer, or

## NOTES

*Consider attending a deep-dive seminar online over a weekend to discuss this material on Jesus and develop your own habits of delight and worship! Search for "Online Seminars" on our website.*

prophet! They stand in awe of Him! How about you?

Write two or three statements here about how good and awesome He is in your own words:

________________________________________

________________________________________

________________________________________

Take two or three of your favorite worship statements from the last eleven days out on a thirty-minute walk and tell Jesus how awesome He is. See if you aren't in an amazing place emotionally and faith-wise when you get back!

## NOTES

Use this page as extra space for your notes and thoughts.

NOTES

# DAY 12
## Discovery

PETER TRIES TO CONTROL JESUS

*When Jesus came to the region of Caesarea Philippi, he asked his disciples, "Who do people say the Son of Man is?" They replied, "Some say John the Baptist; others say Elijah; and still others, Jeremiah or one of the prophets." "But what about you?" he asked. "Who do you say I am?" Simon Peter answered, "You are the Messiah, the Son of the living God." Jesus replied, "Blessed are you, Simon son of Jonah, for this was not revealed to you by flesh and blood, but by my Father in heaven. Matt 16:13-17*

*Then Jesus made it clear to his disciples that it was now necessary for him to go to Jerusalem, submit to an ordeal of suffering at the hands of the religious leaders, be killed, and then on the third day be raised up alive. Peter took him in hand, protesting, "Impossible, Master! That can never be!" But Jesus didn't swerve. "Peter, get out of my way. Satan, get lost. You have no idea how God works." Then Jesus went to work on his disciples. "Anyone who intends to come with me has to let me lead. You're not in the driver's seat; I am. Don't run from suffering; embrace it. Follow me and I'll show you how." Matt 16:21-25 (MSG)*

Wow, Peter must have been losing his mind to take Jesus aside and begin rebuking Him! Once again, Jesus must have been way more **approachable** than we imagine for Peter to even consider doing this.

*From that time on Jesus began to explain to his disciples that he must go to Jerusalem and suffer many things at the hands of the elders, the chief priests and the teachers of the law, and that he must be killed and on the third day be raised to life. Peter took him aside and began to rebuke him. "Never, Lord!" he said. "This shall never happen to you!" Jesus turned and said to Peter, "Get behind me, Satan! You are a stumbling block to me; you do not have in mind the concerns of God, but merely human concerns." Then Jesus said to his disciples, "Whoever wants to be my disciple must deny themselves and take up their cross and follow me. For whoever wants to save their life will lose it, but whoever loses their life for me will find it." Matt 16:21-25*

*But when Jesus turned and looked at His disciples, he rebuked Peter. "Get behind me, Satan!" Mark 8:33*

This attack of the Devil through Peter is just an extension of the Devil's attacks against Jesus in Matthew 4:8-9.

Why is Peter confronting Jesus? What is at stake for Peter? Talk about Peter's possible expectations of Jesus given the two things he identifies about Jesus in the first passage. Consider Matthew 4:1-11 for a connection here (especially the last temptation). Why do you think Jesus is so forceful with His words to Peter? How would you feel if you were Peter? Knowing that Jesus is always good, what is He doing with Peter and the other eleven disciples?

NOTES

## THOUGHTS

First, consider the initial passage and identify the two things that Peter realizes about Jesus. Take a moment and compare and contrast them on the line below and in the margins.

---

Peter hears directly from the Father that Jesus is not only the Messiah, a human earthly ruler like King David, but that He is also the Son of God and is therefore divine. These are two separate truths about Jesus' identity. Israel knew that many prophecies foretold that a good shepherd and ruler was coming to restore the physical kingdom to Israel like in the time of David. However, it was not well known that this anointed one would also be God in human form. Hold on to those two truths.

(As a side point, did you notice that Jesus radically praises Peter for hearing from the Father? The first time I saw this I was shocked that Jesus complimented someone. My image of God was mostly constructed around God telling me to do more, act better, and be more moral. I had no context whatever for Jesus praising and complimenting imperfect sinful people. This was wonderful when I realized Jesus was changing my image of God Himself!)

The next passage describes Jesus telling the disciples that He will be betrayed by the Jewish leaders and priests, be killed, and rise from the dead with a physical body on the third day. Peter reacts and confronts Jesus saying, "No, Lord, this will never happen to You!" It is very probable that Peter is really worried about Jesus. This is dire news. It is also probable that Peter had very developed expectations of Jesus, as the Messiah, showing up like King David and overthrowing Rome to free his Jewish people. This expectation is being gravely threatened by Jesus' announcement of His own death. Further, it is very possible that Peter has plans that he would also rise to national prominence alongside Jesus and fulfill his conclusion that he, himself, is the greatest of the disciples given their obsession with their position (Mark 9-10; Luke 22). Peter's thoughts may have been summarized: "Jesus, You are going to the top, and I am coming with You!"

A combination of these things is probably motivating Peter to do the unthinkable! He takes the Master Himself in hand and begins to intensely confront and rebuke Jesus! When you see this clearly, you begin shaking your head in sheer unbelief at Peter. Peter doesn't realize that he is treading on truly holy ground. Jesus is intending to sacrifice Himself to free humans from the consequences of evil. Either Jesus goes to the cross and is killed to pay for the sins of human beings, or else every human pays for their own sins forever in hell. Peter, under the influence of Satan, is attacking the most precious thing God has ever done for the human race!

## NOTES

*Old Testament Link*

*Peter's resisting and attacking Jesus' mission on the earth reminds me of Moses failing to merely speak to the rock as God commanded to bring water out a second time for the thirsty Israelites. Peter didn't trust Jesus and His plan, and Moses didn't trust God and His plan. "Because you didn't trust in me enough...." Moses breaks God's plan to create a picture of Jesus as the Rock, whom we can merely speak to and receive the provision (water) of forgiveness and the indwelling Holy Spirit! Jesus disciplines Peter without rejection, and God disciplines Moses without rejection. He can't go into the Promised Land, but he's not rejected in relationship with God. He was secure with God and highly honored. Remember, Moses shows up with Elijah when Jesus is*

Stop for a moment and consider, "What if Jesus were passive?" We know some of the dangers of angry, controlling leaders. But what about passive sins? What about just quitting or looking the other way? What if Jesus did what Peter was actually suggesting and chose to protect Himself? Not a single human being would have escaped hell. There would have been no mercy for humans. Every human would be 100 percent accountable for every action, every spoken word, and even every thought. The cross of Jesus was crucial for forgiving humans! God punished Jesus instead of us for every evil action, word, or thought! Thank God for Jesus' fierceness and strength!

Did you read the Matthew 4:1-11 passage I suggested? Do you see any correlation between Satan's final temptation and Peter's actions? Satan comes to Jesus saying that he will give Jesus all the kingdoms of the world if Jesus will worship him, similar to Adam and Eve turning away from God to the Devil. The kingdoms of the world represent people. Satan is trying to tempt Jesus to take a faulty, lying shortcut that bypasses the Cross to save all the people. Peter is doing the same thing. He is being influenced by the Devil to get Jesus to think about himself and his own life rather than lay His life down to save all humans who turn to Him. That's why Jesus calls him a stumbling block. I just want you to see that this event with Peter is a continuation of Satan's temptation of Jesus. It's intense that the Devil uses Jesus' closest friend.

Jesus disciplines Peter instantly with the words, *"Get behind me Satan, you have in mind the things of men, not of God."* Now, I don't know about you, but I don't want to be called "Satan" by anyone, but especially not Jesus! Wow! But we realize Peter is not Satan. Jesus is delivering a very, very strong correction for His chief follower. Notice that the passage in Mark says that Jesus turns and looks at the other eleven disciples. He is also addressing them and their inner thought lives. This is the most severe moment of Jesus' correction and discipline that I have found in the Gospels relative to the disciples. That is one of the reasons we need to process it so thoroughly.

Years ago, I would wilt under this passage because my image of God was so distorted and tortured with fear and rejection. I just could not understand this passage in a healthy way. All I could see was Jesus ripping Peter to pieces for no good reason. Peter was just worried about Jesus dying, right? However, now with a more accurate image of God, can we see what Jesus is doing here? Is He rejecting Peter here? No! Does He take away Peter's leadership position? No! Does He reject Peter personally? No! Then what is Jesus doing?

Jesus is severely disciplining Peter for trying to take control of the Father's will and the Father's agenda for Jesus and humankind! Peter wants to be in the driver's seat! Peter wants to control Jesus according to his own reasoning and expectations of what Jesus, as the Messiah, should be doing. And it most certainly does not include Jesus dying! We all want to do things our own way and control Jesus. We don't want to say it, but it's true. Jesus knows this is bad for us and the people around us. The best way is for us to learn to truly follow Jesus and do exactly as He instructs. Peter isn't the Master; Jesus is! If Peter and the others are going to be good pastors and leaders of the sheep, they must learn to follow Jesus rather than their own reasoning. Jesus' strong correction and discipline are painful for Peter, but they are for his own good!

We all know what is going to happen if Peter runs his own life. Peter, just like all of us, needs Jesus to direct and lead and grow him. How many times have I said (and you have probably said), "God, this is crazy! I don't need to do that. I need to go over here and do this! How can You be so confused!" We trust in our own faulty reasoning and forget how limited our brains are and how inaccurately they perceive reality.

Therefore Jesus, in the next breath, gives the message about "lose your own life to find your life." This is completely connected to Peter rebuking Jesus! He is telling them that if they really want to find their lives and what is good for them and those they love, they have to submit to Jesus' leadership! They can't find goodness on their own. If they pursue their own reasoning and expectations, they will lose their lives and their best selves and make a wreck of their lives. (And you can see this in people's lives all around us who insist on doing life on their own terms, whether they say they are Christians or not.)

This verse about "lose your own life to find your life" used to be my most hated verse in the Bible! (Is it ok that I am honest and tell you I had a most hated verse?) I hated it because my picture of God was so twisted by fear that I interpreted this verse, thinking God wants to take away everything that I love and give me a life of everything that I hate. I thought He was calling me to be miserable. To be completely honest, my image of God was laced with character elements that were more true of the Devil than God! That is truly what the Devil wants. He wants to give us lives of pain and misery. However, Jesus wants to give us abundant lives of joy and goodness (John 10:10). It is for that reason that Jesus tells us the way to find our lives, and that is by letting go of what we think we want to do and follow the only One who is good, because He will lead us to joy!

So, even after Peter specifically fails and sins through trying to control Jesus, because of his own desires for prominence and his expectations of the Messiah, Jesus still doesn't reject or shame Peter! Jesus intensely disciplines Peter to once again get Peter to follow Him no matter what happens for Peter's good and the good of all people. What does I Corinthians 13:7-8 say? Love always protects, love always perseveres, and love never fails. Jesus knows that Peter's own way is not the best for him nor his community but following Jesus will lead Peter to his best life! There is a place to say, "Jesus, I am so grateful that You don't let me just ruin my life doing it according to my own faulty thinking, but You resist my foolishness and draw me into Your path for my life! Thank You for Your goodness to me!"

## TAKEAWAY

*"The glory of Christ, who is the image of God"* (2 Cor 4:4). Since Jesus is the image of God, what do you see in His response to Peter that brings you new insight about God's character? What is the significance of this for you as you process your expectations of what God should do or not do in your life? What about your need for Jesus' leadership in your life? It is so important to write things down and slowly process.

## NOTES

transfigured in Luke 9:28-29. Moses made it to the true "Promised Land."

(Exodus 17:1-7 water out of the rock the 1st time; Numbers 20 water out of the rock the 2nd time.)

**NOTES**

Jesus is telling Peter to get out of the driver's seat of his life and get in the passenger seat and actively follow Jesus' lead for his good and the good of the world. Jesus disciplines Peter and the other disciples but without rejection; this reveals that God also disciplines His children entirely without rejection! This radical security with God, revealed by Jesus, gives us the confidence to grow from God's correction rather than lose heart! It is the enemy who attacks us with accusation, condemnation, and the fear of rejection to tear us down. Jesus reveals that God works with us patiently bringing us into alignment with Him (repentance) to build us up! We become greater lovers of people! This makes us delight in Him all the more!

## FIRST COMMANDMENT PRAYER

Jesus, I was so confused about who You are! Half the things I feared about Your character were more true of the enemy than of You! I was always afraid You were rejecting me when I failed or sinned. The more I see that You never rejected Peter or the disciples when they sinned gives me confidence to come close to You! I want to know how "to run to You" instead of "run from You" when I fail and sin ! You know, I think You might be better than I thought You were! Help me delight in You and worship You passionately!

### WORSHIP WITHOUT MUSIC

This verse continues to come to mind:

> *My son, do not make light of the Lord's discipline, and do not lose heart when He rebukes you, because the Lord disciplines the one He loves and chastens everyone He accepts as His son. Heb 12:5*

If you are like me, can you relate to being completely overwhelmed by Jesus' discipline? Contrast how you have felt by other people's dysfunctional discipline rather than Jesus' healthy discipline for Peter? Write down two or three lines to Jesus telling Him how good, healthy, and wonderful His discipline for Peter is!

________________________________________

________________________________________

________________________________________

*Do you like Facebook or Instagram? Search for "God Is Just Like Jesus" and encourage us!*

## NOTES

Use this page as extra space for your notes and thoughts.

NOTES

# DAY 13 Discovery

## WHO IS THE GREATEST AT THE LAST SUPPER?

> *After taking the cup, he gave thanks and said, "Take this and divide it among you. For I tell you I will not drink again from the fruit of the vine until the kingdom of God comes." And he took bread, gave thanks and broke it, and gave it to them, saying, "This is my body given for you; do this in remembrance of me." Luke 22:17-19*

> *A dispute also arose among them as to which of them was considered to be greatest. Jesus said to them, "The kings of the Gentiles lord it over them; and those who exercise authority over them call themselves Benefactors. But you are not to be like that. Instead, the greatest among you should be like the youngest, and the one who rules like the one who serves. For who is greater, the one who is at the table or the one who serves? Is it not the one who is at the table? But I am among you as one who serves. You are those who have stood by me in my trials. And I confer on you a kingdom, just as my Father conferred one on me, so that you may eat and drink at my table in my kingdom and sit on thrones, judging the twelve tribes of Israel." Luke 22:24-30*

Wow, really? At the Last Supper? Guys, come on!

> *So he got up from the meal, took off his outer clothing, and wrapped a towel around his waist. After that, he poured water into a basin and began to wash his disciples' feet, drying them with the towel that was wrapped around him.... When he had finished washing their feet, he put on his clothes and returned to his place. "Do you understand what I have done for you?" he asked them. "You call me 'Teacher' and 'Lord,' and rightly so, for that is what I am. Now that I, your Lord and Teacher, have washed your feet, you also should wash one another's feet." John 13:4-5, 12-14*

Boy, sounds like me...so self-confident...such pride. I'm so grateful Jesus deals kindly with Peter's arrogance. Maybe He will with my pride too.

So, what is the significance of this particular meal? What tradition did Jesus institute here? Right after this, what happens among the disciples for, at least, the third time? Given all of this, how would have you responded? How does Jesus respond?

________________________________________

________________________________________

### THOUGHTS

What an epic night! Jesus, just hours before He is betrayed to the Chief Priest and the Romans, gives the disciples the sacrament of communion, the bread and the wine of Jesus' sacrifice for them and for us! Then, shortly after, the argument erupts again, "Which of us is the greatest?" It's hard to image they could ignore Jesus' previous instruction and challenge on this point. But it is deep within them (and us). I can imagine some of the things that might be said, "I'm the greatest! I walked on water while the rest of you were afraid to get out of the boat!" James might respond, "Yeah, but you sank. Jesus called us the Sons of Thunder! That's the kind of power we walk in! Besides we were with Jesus when He was transformed, revealing His true power and glory! Meanwhile you other disciples couldn't even get a demon out of the boy at the bottom of the mountain." They might respond, "Well, at least we weren't trying

NOTES

to use God's power to wipe out an entire Samaritan village! Jesus sure rebuked you two!"

This continual argument is core to human nature. This is the core issue of Hollywood: who's the best, who's the most beautiful, who can throw the biggest party, or who has the most power? This is often the core issue in sports as some of the football players, basketball players, or Olympians pound their chests or fist pump the air exclaiming that they are the strongest or fastest! How many of us have sat in corporate C-Level Executive meetings as the pushing, pulling, and manipulation breaks out as those in the meeting force one another into submission and showcase themselves as the greatest? It's ugly, but that's life all across the world. Jesus is teaching us to reach for something different.

So, once again I will ask, how would you have responded to repetitive prideful sins in others? How do you look at yourself and treat yourself after repetitive failures and sins? Please use the Notes column to answer these two questions.

You would think at this point, with all the impending stress of Jesus' imminent betrayal, capture, abuse by the Roman soldiers, and crucifixion, Jesus would have had enough! The drama and stress would have been way too much for any human to manage. When you consider that He was tempted in all ways like we are (Heb 4:15), consider also that He might have been tempted to despair by the disciples failing in pride and competition right before He dies. What would you have done? How do you respond when you are under tremendous life-threatening pressures and those closest to you fail and sin? I can imagine myself melting down and shouting at the disciples and accusing them of sin and failing me as I am terrified of my impending torture and death. A friend of mine named Elijah said, "If I were Jesus, I would have done the Darth Vader neck pinch on them all!" Someone else said, "If that was a Pharisee instead of Jesus, there would not have been washing of feet but whipping and lashing!" It all just goes to highlight how amazing Jesus is!

But there is more. How do we even describe the stress involved in the supernatural truth that the sins of all human beings, past, present and future, will be laid on Jesus' soul as God punishes Him, instead of us, for our sin? It's an act of total justice against evil so that God can forgive whoever will turn to Him in mercy. It's ultimate pressure, and Jesus doesn't crack, nor does He lose it and vent on the disciples. Nor does He get angry. He doesn't even get depressed. (Have you ever considered the glorious self-control of Jesus? It's the ninth fruit of the Spirit in Galatians 5.)

However, let's be clear about the cost to Jesus. It takes a tremendous toll on Him. The Message Bible says Jesus *"was visibly upset"* (John 13:21) when He predicted someone at the table would betray Him. Also in Gethsemane Jesus says, *"My soul is overwhelmed with sorrow to the point of death!"* (Matt 26:38). So the cost and stress to Jesus was astronomical!

With epic patience Jesus instructs the disciples again on the core issue of Christian leadership. *"The kings of the Gentiles lord it over them...but you are not to be like that."* James and John were wanting to sit at the left and right of Jesus to be honored above

**NOTES**

*Old Testament Link*
*The disciples' sins of pride and arrogance and Jesus serving them by cleaning them up remind me of Joshua's sin. Satan accuses him, but the Lord serves him and removes his filthy clothes and puts a clean turban on his head. Forgiveness! Zechariah 3*

all, but Jesus was wanting to show them how to serve everyday people in their need. Service and humility are to be the marks of a Christian leader, not hierarchy and who's at the top of the food chain! Who's preaching the message? Who's honored on the platform? How many pastors and lay leaders (including ourselves) have violated this exact commandment? Sometimes we just want to be the CEO of the church and delegate tasks to accomplish our vision, but Jesus didn't call us to that. He was calling the leaders to actually serve real people in the church with real needs. Church, meet corporate America! (It's a sad reality.) However, we can do better than that when we truly follow Him.

Once again it is critical to ask how Jesus responded, and He did not accuse the disciples of sin and reject them! Jesus doesn't even shame them! What does He do?

Jesus goes even further than patient instruction. He uses Himself as the ultimate example. *"But I am among you as one who serves."* Jesus, who can single-handedly confront the entire Jewish leadership structure, who can heal the blind, call a shoal of fish into Peter's net, and raise the dead, stoops low and puts each word into practice. He takes off his outer garment, kneels on the ground, and He begins to wash their feet (John 13:1). They are shocked and overwhelmed! This is a visceral experience beyond anything that they have ever understood! No world religious leader has ever done anything like this. Jesus is the utterly Unique One in all of human history! The God-Man stoops to serve His followers and wash their dry, cracked, and dirty feet after having trodden the hot roads of Israel! Peter can't even handle it, *"'No,' Peter said, 'You shall never wash my feet'"* (John 13:8).

It is shocking, and perhaps even scandalizing, but Jesus' humility and service to wash the disciples' feet reveal God's heart of humility and service as He washes sin and evil from the hearts of all humans who will respond to Him.

Let's be clear. Jesus didn't "put on" humility for a moment to teach the disciples to be humble. No! Humility is at the core of His divine identity. He is and always will be humble! During his days as a human and all the eternal ages to come, He will always and forever be truly humble!

Jesus stands in stark contrast to other leaders of world religions.

A friend named Janine said, "It's almost like He removes his outer layer to reveal His internal life and character of humility and show Himself to us!"

Let's just drive this home with yet one more passage. Read Luke 12:35-38. Here I will just quote verse 37:

> *"It will be good for those servants whose master finds them watching when he comes. I tell you the truth, he will dress himself to serve, will have them recline at the table and will come and wait on them."*

That is a shocking verse. Did you read what it said? Take a moment and read the entire passage and then write in the Notes column what it means for you before you go any further.

NOTES

This radical verse confirms that humility is at the core of Jesus' eternal identity! That also means that humility is at the core of the Father's eternal identity. Now that's the glory of God! Some think that the radiant light around God is the most impressive aspect of His glory. It's amazing, but the character of God the Father is His true Glory! One of the ways that Jesus will reward us for faithful service to God's people is that He will come and serve us at a banquet feast! Once again, understanding that, you feel like Peter did when he said in unbelief to Jesus, *"Lord, are you going to wash my feet?"* But it confirms what we are saying about the hidden identity of the Father, of the Son and of the Holy Spirit. Each is humble in their own rights. The Devil is always trying to be the CEO, the celebrated celebrity, or the top dog. He tries to get everyone to serve his wicked and selfish desires. However, God is so different! Father, Son, and Spirit are ultimately powerful but radically humble and will be all through the Resurrection and the infinite ages to come! When the disciples are arguing about who is the greatest, Jesus is merely answering and saying, "Don't do it that way, become 'just like Me'!"

At the end of the age, it will be a conflict between two houses of worship. People will choose to worship the Beast or Jesus. The Beast will trample the earth with war and economic control and oppression as he seeks to the be the greatest. Jesus, as the Lion and the Lamb, will hammer the Beast's kingdom with the seals, trumpets and bowls, and serve those who are faithful to Him to resist the Beast and overcome his wickedness! Who you worship will be the central issue.

If you have seen Jesus, you have seen God! No other founder of a great religion comes near the greatness, humility, and power of Jesus, the Messiah! They all have had elements of His matchless goodness and character, but the fullness can only be found in Jesus! Meditating on the God-Man will release delight and worship in your heart that will erupt in words and praise out loud!

## TAKEAWAY

*"'No one has ever seen God, but the one and only Son, who is himself God and is in closest relationship with the Father, has made him known'"* (John 1:18). Since Jesus has made the Father known, what does this passage reveal to you about the Father? What does this mean to you that Jesus washes your feet in middle of your sin?

---

Jesus' wonderfully patient instruction to mature the disciples is evident even when their competition occurs again, on the very last night before Jesus dies! Jesus' mind-blowing patience reveals the Father's patience to grow and develop the disciples. Jesus reveals how He has been serving the disciples (and all of us) throughout their lives by the physical experience of washing their feet. It is the picture of God the Father and the Holy Spirit reaching down to human beings drowning in hatred, bitterness, lust, and jealousy and washing us free of such things and drawing us into deeper experiences of joy, wholeness, goodness, and peace!

NOTES

### FIRST COMMANDMENT PRAYER

Jesus, You are the very image of God! It is amazing how You continue to bear with the disciples' sin of selfish ambition and competition on the very last night before You died! Anyone else would have had a meltdown and started yelling – but not You! Your patience and goodness are without comparison in any religion. And Your humility, infused with strength, is incredibly beautiful beyond compare! I delight to worship You, but I also want to become just like You!

### WORSHIP WITHOUT MUSIC

Have you ever been in a high pressure, high stakes situation where you felt like everything was on the line and you were trying to communicate something radically important? Then a few people, because of their own pride, derail your entire message? How would you feel about that?

________________________________________

________________________________________

Can you relate (at least try) to the tremendous stress Jesus was under, knowing He would soon die, and having someone sin a repetitive sin that you have confronted them with on numerous times?

How differently does Jesus respond to the "Who is the greatest?" argument for the third time than we would?

Enjoy and delight in Jesus' good character and write a few statements directly to Him:

________________________________________

________________________________________

Take your top ten worship statements out on a fifteen-to thirty-minute prayer walk (with or without music) and worship Him! Or take time to journal "to" Him, not just about Him. Or create art (watercolors, oil paints, sketching) with your top ten worship statements. Creating space to focus on Him alone will deepen your connection with Jesus and touch the real identity issues in your life. Engage with Him!

*Audio podcasts are a great way to review this material and be reminded of how good Jesus is! It's perfect for a workout, commuting, or cleaning the house or garage. Search for "God Is Just Like Jesus" on Apple Podcasts, Spotify, or Amazon Music.*

## NOTES

Use this page as extra space for your notes and thoughts.

NOTES

We don't even know our own positive potential nor our own sinfulness. Ouch!

# DAY 14 Discovery

IS PETER THE GREATEST?

*"You will all fall away," Jesus told them, "for it is written: 'I will strike the shepherd, and the sheep will be scattered.' But after I have risen, I will go ahead of you into Galilee." Peter declared, "Even if all fall away, I will not." "Truly I tell you," Jesus answered, "today–yes, tonight–before the rooster crows twice you yourself will disown me three times." But Peter insisted emphatically, "Even if I have to die with you, I will never disown you." And all the others said the same. Mark 14:27-31*

*Jesus told them, "You're all going to feel that your world is falling apart and that it's my fault. There's a Scripture that says, I will strike the shepherd; The sheep will go helter-skelter. But after I am raised up, I will go ahead of you, leading the way to Galilee." Peter blurted out, "Even if everyone else is ashamed of you when things fall to pieces, I won't be." Jesus said, "Don't be so sure. Today, this very night in fact, before the rooster crows twice, you will deny me three times." He blustered in protest, "Even if I have to die with you, I will never deny you." All the others said the same thing. Mark 14:27-31 (MSG)*

*"Simon, Simon, Satan has asked to sift all of you as wheat. But I have prayed for you, Simon...." Luke 22:31-32*

How is Peter continuing the argument about which of them is the greatest? How does Peter feel about himself compared to the other disciples? Does Jesus accuse Peter of sin? If not, what does Jesus do? Put it in your own words.

________________________________________________________

________________________________________________________

## THOUGHTS

This is a very powerful and emotional passage. Jesus tells Peter that he is not going to be loyal to Him when the pressure is on and that he is going to "fall away." Peter can't believe it! Jesus goes on to say that Satan is going to tempt him and will be successful, to a degree.

How does Peter respond? His response is the outworking of the four-fold argument of "which one of us is the greatest?" In Mark 14:31 it says, *"Peter insisted emphatically, 'Even if I have to die with you, I will never disown you.' And all the others said the same."* However, Peter goes further in pride. *"Peter replied, 'Even if all fall away on account of You, I never will'"* (Matt 26:33). Peter is radically convinced that He is the greatest!

Peter lacks humility and the self-awareness of his sinful nature. Peter is saying to himself, "No way! This isn't going to happen! I'm better than that! In fact I'm better than the rest of these guys! They might be disloyal to You, Jesus, but I never will!" (my paraphrase). Peter has a deep lack of knowledge about his own human nature. However, and more importantly, he also has a deep lack of knowledge about Jesus' profound love and provision for himself.

I also want to note that the sifting that Jesus talks about relative to the Devil has to do with Peter's pride and this argument about which of them is the greatest. Jesus has promised that they will sit on thrones. But they are going to get there by serving, not by bossing everyone else around and being on the top of the hierarchy or leadership structure! They are going to be great; they just don't understand how they are going to get there. Peter's pride is setting himself up for a huge failure. And Satan is going to try to use this fall to cover Peter with condemnation, shame, and an untrue perception of rejection. Satan wants to try to separate Peter from Jesus. It's not going to work, but that is the enemy's attack plan. Peter's defense and ours is Jesus' actions on our behalf, "I have prayed for you," and knowing His good character pushes off the condemnation and shame and encourages us to trust Jesus.

You would hardly believe that this internal arrogance and pride about being the greatest could fully survive inside Peter after Jesus, the God-Man, kneels down and washes each of their feet. You would think that would have obliterated this desire! However, it's not quite over yet.

How would you have responded to Peter, after you washed his feet, as he declares that he is better than all the rest of the disciples? How would a Pharisee have responded? How about one of those old, but well-meaning, Holiness preachers? How about a grouchy Catholic nun (there are great nuns, but just asking the question to include everyone)? How about a crusty Orthodox priest? Write out your raw thoughts and feelings in the Notes column.

After they said, "No, we won't deny you," I would have probably said, "Oh, yes you will! I'll be suffering on my own, and you guys will all be together, safe and sound." Then I would have a big emotional pity party for myself (privately). It's emotional blackmail. I'm not proud of it. However, Jesus' emotional health is so much healthier than mine! Duh!

Also consider that Jesus was tempted in every way as we are. He could have been tempted to despair at Peter's pride, concluding that he was going to be loyal to Jesus when the other disciples would run in fear. Jesus could have been tempted with thoughts like, *Has it all been a waste, these last three years?*

Young preachers like to preach the "Do Better" message and the "Try Harder" message. When they see sin, they preach "do more" and "perform better morally." Interestingly, that is not what Jesus does here.

How does Jesus actually respond to Peter? You would think that after He washes their feet and Peter is still obsessed with being the greatest, Jesus would finally have melted down! But no! Even then Jesus is steady and patient. Does He react like someone who is mostly influenced by world culture or the Devil's emotions? Does He fault-find, accuse, and shame Peter? No! Even though Peter is still poised in pride, thinking he

**NOTES**

**Old Testament Link**

The disciples' wrestling with pride continues to remind me of Old Testament saints who wrestled repeatedly with different sins like fear. Jesus constantly instructs the disciples about this sin. Joshua is wrestling with fear after Moses dies. That is why God instructs him over and over to "be strong, be courageous." Joshua 1 especially v6, 7, 8

NOTES

is way better than the other disciples, Jesus remains calm and patiently instructs him. The struggle with division in their midst, just like many churches and organizations, is still very much alive.

Jesus patiently instructs Peter about his weakness and sin. There is no fault-finding. There is no condemnation. Jesus is giving Peter information about himself so that when he commits these sins he will know that it didn't catch Jesus by surprise. This means that the love and commitment that Jesus has for Peter is not renegotiated because new information appears about Peter's weaknesses. No, Jesus knew it all along. Peter can be confident since Jesus loved him before it happened and Jesus loves Peter after it happened. Since Jesus knew Peter would sin in this way before it happened, then Jesus' love for him is still intact. He is absolutely amazing! And again, doesn't the urge to just tell Jesus how awesome He is just arise in your heart? Speak that out and give yourself to worship whether you have music around you or not!

### TAKEAWAY

*"The Son is the image of the invisible God"* (Col 1:15). Since Jesus is the image of God, what does His response to Peter show you about the Father? Have you ever been utterly convinced you were going to come through for someone, only to horribly fail later? What does Jesus' response to Peter mean for you?

---

Jesus knows that Peter is going to fail and deny Him. Jesus patiently instructs Peter and the other ten disciples so they will know this didn't catch Him off guard. It might be new information to them, but this isn't new information to Jesus. Therefore Jesus' love for them before the sin and after the sin is the same! This reveals God's love for the disciples as well! The Father works with you and me in the same way during our sins and failures. We can know this is how God relates to us because Jesus is the perfect image of the Father!

### FIRST COMMANDMENT PRAYER

Jesus, Your love and goodness continue time and time again after many failures and sins on Peter's part and on my part. I love knowing that, because I have failures and sins which I struggle with on a repetitive basis. Cause me to know how You help me so that I can run to You instead of from You when I sin! How else can I grow strong enough to overcome my sin? Do I really think I can fix myself? Foolishness! Help me to know You and how You relate to me and thereby war against my sin and overcome – to become "just like You!"

NOTES

## WORSHIP WITHOUT MUSIC

What do you feel as you look at Peter filled with arrogance, arguing for the fourth time, absolutely convinced that he is stronger and more faithful than all the rest? Can you remember a time or two when you were very proud? Compare how Jesus responds to Peter with how people have responded to your sin. Write down two or three things you like, love, or treasure about Jesus here:

_______________________________________________

_______________________________________________

*If you haven't tried our online discussions, consider attending just two and see if you don't love them. Search for "Online Discussions" on www.GodIsJustLikeJesus.com*

NOTES

# DAY 15
## Discovery

THEY ALL FALL ASLEEP

*After He said these things, Jesus became visibly upset, and then He told them why. "One of you is going to betray Me." John 13:21 (MSG)*

*Then Jesus went with his disciples to a place called Gethsemane, and he said to them, "Sit here while I go over there and pray." He took Peter and the two sons of Zebedee along with him, and he began to be sorrowful and troubled. Then he said to them, "My soul is overwhelmed with sorrow to the point of death. Stay here and keep watch with me." Going a little farther, he fell with his face to the ground and prayed, "My Father, if it is possible, may this cup be taken from me. Yet not as I will, but as you will." Then he returned to his disciples and found them sleeping. "Couldn't you men keep watch with me for one hour?" he asked Peter. "Watch and pray so that you will not fall into temptation. The spirit is willing, but the flesh is weak." He went away a second time and prayed, "My Father, if it is not possible for this cup to be taken away unless I drink it, may your will be done." When he came back, he again found them sleeping, because their eyes were heavy. So he left them and went away once more and prayed the third time, saying the same thing. Then he returned to the disciples and said to them, "Are you still sleeping and resting? Look, the hour has come, and the Son of Man is delivered into the hands of sinners. Rise! Let us go! Here comes my betrayer!" Matt 26:36-46*

*An angel from heaven appeared to him and strengthened him. And being in anguish, he prayed more earnestly, and his sweat was like drops of blood falling to the ground. When he rose from prayer and went back to the disciples, he found them asleep, exhausted from sorrow. Luke 22:43-45*

Wow, "overwhelmed with sorrow." I bet. Those guys sunk their whole lives into Jesus, and now He is leaving.

*He came back and found them sound asleep. He said to Peter, "Simon, you went to sleep on me? Can't you stick it out with me a single hour? Stay alert, be in prayer, so you don't enter the danger zone without even knowing it. Don't be naive. Part of you is eager, ready for anything in God; but another part is as lazy as an old dog sleeping by the fire." He then went back and prayed the same prayer. Returning, he again found them sound asleep. They simply couldn't keep their eyes open, and they didn't have a plausible excuse. He came back a third time and said, "Are you going to sleep all night? No–you've slept long enough. Time's up. The Son of Man is about to be betrayed into the hands of sinners. Get up. Let's get going. My betrayer has arrived." Mark 14:37-42 (MSG)*

This is Jesus' most agonizing hour and His greatest struggle before the cross. How would you have responded to your friends abandoning you in your desperate hour? But even here, how does Jesus respond to the disciples' failure? Are you in awe of Jesus?

______________________________________________

______________________________________________

NOTES

## THOUGHTS

I have included the first verse from John 13 to begin to highlight the strains and stresses on Jesus. Before Jesus tells them that a betrayer exists, He is "visibly upset." That is the way The Message translates this verse. Can you image Jesus "visibly upset"? Judas' betrayal of Jesus was a huge event and really impacted Jesus. We shouldn't minimize this.

Jesus leads the disciples out of the upper room into the Garden of Gethsemane. Jesus asks the eleven disciples (and other disciples) to sit while He goes a little further to pray. He takes Peter, James, and John with Him and asks them, *"Stay here and keep watch with Me."* Jesus wants these three to be with Him as He is struggling in prayer. There is something personal here. Jesus, then, reveals how crushed He is and how sorrowful He is. In fact, Jesus says that He is *"overwhelmed with sorrow to the point of death."* What does it take for the Son of God to be overwhelmed? What does it take for the Son of God to ask mere humans to stay near and keep watch as He processes the mental and emotional anguish regarding His own torture and death?

He is not just overwhelmed, but overwhelmed to the point of death! The pressure and stress that are on Jesus are beyond what we can even imagine. Jesus goes a bit further away and *"fell with His face to the ground"* (Matt 26:39). Do you connect with the great manly figure of Jesus, the Master, falling to the ground? Remember, Jesus has dealt with crowds of desperate people needing healing and deliverance, with confronting the entire Jewish leadership, with raising dead people to life, and with calming a raging storm on the sea! But facing the Father's just and righteous judgment against all human sin that will be laid on His soul causes Him to fall on the ground and then sweat drops of blood. It's not the torture and crucifixion but the righteous punishment against evil that He will bear in His own body and soul that brings Him to His knees. Mark 14:35 says, He *"prayed that if possible the hour might pass from Him."* Luke 22:43 says the struggle was so intense that, *"An angel from heaven appeared to him and strengthened him. And being in anguish He prayed all the more earnestly."* An angel actually shows up and strengthens Him. But what is the result? Jesus is in "anguish" because the struggle is so great! He uses the new strength to pray all the harder! He is wrestling and struggling to a degree that is hard for us to even understand! And He did it for us and everyone who would call on His name in this world! When He returns from His dire wrestling, Jesus finds that the three disciples have fallen asleep out of sheer exhaustion and grief (Luke 22:45). *"They didn't know what to say to Him"* (Mark 14:40).

Unfortunately, the disciples fail to stand by Jesus in Gethsemane! They are exhausted from sorrow because Jesus has said that He will go away. Their whole lives for the last three years have swirled around the God-Man. Now He says that He is going away! They are shaken and filled with raw grief and fear. What will they do? What will life be like? What will the Pharisees do? What will the Romans do? All three of them fall asleep rather than watch with Him as He sets His soul to endure death on a Roman cross!

**NOTES**

*Old Testament Link*
*The disciples' being worn out, giving up, and going to sleep remind me of David being worn out with Saul chasing him and losing faith in God to protect him, and then running away to the land of the Philistines and settling in Ziklag.*
*1 Samuel 27:1*

*Jesus challenges and instructs the disciples, and they recover and lead the church. David "finds strength in the Lord." He recovers everything and shortly after becomes King over all Israel.*
*1 Samuel 30:6*

Well, when you read Jesus' questions to the disciples, have you partly cleaned up your picture of Jesus' character from accusation yet? Or do you still mostly hear fault-finding or something else in the questions He asks His disciples about falling asleep. Since we know Jesus is never going to reject His followers, we know it must be something else.

Jesus says to Peter, *"Couldn't you keep watch for one hour? Watch and pray so that you will not fall into temptation. The spirit is willing, but the flesh is weak."* He is basically saying, "Stay awake and pray or else you will be tempted to run and hide when they come to capture Me. But know this, your spirit is willing. Your inner man wants to obey and do this well. But you also need to know that your body is weak and tired, and you may very well pass out from exhaustion. I want you to know that I understand both these things about you, the positive and the negative." This is basic instruction and a challenge for the disciples. They can do this, but they are really going to have to seek God for the strength to press on with sweat and tears.

Someone asked, "What is He telling them to pray about?" It is important to realize there is more than one way to fulfill the Scriptures' prediction that they will all fall away and Jesus' prediction that Peter will deny knowing Him. Therefore Jesus' exhortation to "watch and pray," if obeyed, might have lessened the depths of Peter's denial of Jesus with oaths and curses. It might have helped Peter overcome the sense of guilt, failure, and shame the Devil was trying to heap on him. It's just a thought.

Jesus comes back after the third prayer and says, *"Are you still sleeping and resting? Enough! The hour has come. Look, the Son of Man is delivered into the hands of sinners."* This statement combined with the previous one raises the bar from instruction to challenge and correction. Again, Jesus doesn't reject them, but He does bring some intense challenge and correction. He knows that they have failed to stay vigilant and will not be as resistant to fear once the Romans come to capture Him. Jesus needs them to learn to focus since they will be leading the entire church soon. He isn't attacking them, but He is demanding that they grow for their good and the good of the people they will lead. And it's the same for us and those we will influence.

Now, let's flip the coin to the other side. It is so painful to even ask, what would a worldly leader, a Pharisee, or Satan say at a moment of failure like this? You can almost hear the accusation: "I needed you, and you failed to come through and support me!" Or what about shame? "After all I invested in you over the last three years, and you fail during the most critical moment!" Or what about rejection, "After all I'm about to do for you, can't you stay awake for me? Forget leading the church. You'll never make it."

I can't imagine the pressure and agony Jesus was facing. It is times like this when I blow my top the most and get the most angry with the failure of other people. Usually at these times I not only resort to accusations and shaming, but I obsess on it! I am very vulnerable to trying to motivate people with the Devil's methods. How about you? Jesus, however, is not like that. He is so amazingly different! Even when the pressures of the entire human race are bearing down on Him, He acts with goodness and works to grow the disciples and reveal the Father!

NOTES

Peter, James, and John fail to stay by Jesus' side and pray for their own strength right at His most critical hour. Jesus loves them and coaches them to become stronger for their new leadership tasks for the fledgling church. Jesus is the Rock, and His character is solid and unchanging! He is utterly amazing!

## TAKEAWAY

*"'The one who looks at me is seeing the one who sent me'"* (John 12:45). The verse says that if you look at Jesus, you are seeing God. Therefore, what did you see in Jesus' attitude toward the disciples in Gethsemane, and what does that show you about God? Have you ever failed Jesus? What is the significance of this in your own life?

---

Even during Jesus' greatest agonies, He refuses to attack, accuse, or condemn those who fail Him. Even then Jesus instructs, challenges, and corrects His followers to make them greater because that is exactly what His Father does with Him. Jesus never experienced the Father motivating Him in dysfunctional ways; therefore, Jesus always relates to the disciples in emotionally healthy ways. God, the Son, perfectly reflects God the Father!

### FIRST COMMANDMENT PRAYER

Oh Jesus! Knowing that You are not rejecting Peter, James, or John when they greatly fail You helps me have confidence in You, even though I cannot see You with my eyes. Knowing that You will not reject me for my failure or sin really helps me be able to receive Your correction and learn from it rather than run from You! Help me to always trust Your goodness and Your correction so I can grow in the best and most healthy way!

## WORSHIP WITHOUT MUSIC

Have you ever been in a situation where someone has failed you in a critical life-changing moment? How did you react?

---

Compare your response to Jesus' response.

---

NOTES

*For this series on video, search YouTube for "God Is Just Like Jesus."*

Really take some time and write down a number of statements to Jesus about how amazing, awesome, good He is in the face of Peter's failures and sin, and ours:

______________________________________________

______________________________________________

## NOTES

Use this page as extra space for your notes and thoughts.

NOTES

# DAY 16 Discovery

WHAT WAS ON JESUS' FACE WHEN PETER DENIES KNOWING HIM?

> *"Then, Lord," Simon Peter replied, "not just my feet but my hands and my head as well!" Jesus answered, "Those who have had a bath need only to wash their feet, their whole body is clean. And you are clean." John 13:9-10*

> *"Simon, Simon, Satan has asked to sift all of you as wheat. But I have prayed for you, Simon, that your faith may not fail. And when you have turned back, strengthen your brothers." But he replied, "Lord, I am ready to go with you to prison and to death." Jesus answered, "I tell you, Peter, before the rooster crows today, you will deny three times that you know me." Luke 22:31-34*

> *Now Peter was sitting out in the courtyard, and a servant girl came to him. "You also were with Jesus of Galilee," she said. But he denied it before them all. "I don't know what you're talking about," he said. Then he went out to the gateway, where another servant girl saw him and said to the people there, "This fellow was with Jesus of Nazareth." He denied it again, with an oath: "I don't know the man!" After a little while, those standing there went up to Peter and said, "Surely you are one of them; your accent gives you away." Then he began to call down curses, and he swore to them, "I don't know the man!" Immediately a rooster crowed. Then Peter remembered the word Jesus had spoken: "Before the rooster crows, you will disown me three times." And he went outside and wept bitterly. Matt 26:69-74*

> *About an hour later another asserted, "Certainly this fellow was with him, for he is a Galilean." Peter replied, "Man, I don't know what you're talking about!" Just as he was speaking, the rooster crowed. The Lord turned and looked straight at Peter. Luke 22:59-61*

*I've never seen that verse before. I wonder how Jesus' face looked?*

Peter completely fails to show up and stand by Jesus. Jesus knows this in advance. How does Jesus act toward Peter before his immense failure and sin? There are three or four clues in the first two passages.

____________________________________________

____________________________________________

## THOUGHTS

After Jesus' great struggle in the garden, the Roman soldiers appear, led by Judas, to capture Jesus. Peter courageously hacks off the ear of the high priest's servant, but Jesus stops the violence and surrenders to the Romans. They lead Jesus to the house of the high priest. Peter follows at a distance and sits down in the courtyard. Here Jesus' prophecy comes true, and Peter denies that he knows and loves Jesus. Matthew 26:72 and 74 reveals the intensity of Peter's fear and denial. Those verses say Peter denied Jesus with an oath, saying, *"I don't know the man!"* An Old Testament oath would be something like, "May the Lord do something horrible to me if I'm not telling you the

NOTES

truth – I don't know the man!" Verse 74 says, *"Then he began to call down curses on himself and he swore to them, 'I don't know the man.'"* Curses would be even worse. A curse could be something like, "May my life and the lives of my children be cursed with horrible diseases if I'm not telling the truth – I don't know the man!" Oaths and curses reveal the desperation in Peter's heart in this moment.

This is the ultimate failure and sin of Peter's life! And also of the other ten disciples. Please note that the "you" in Luke 22:31 in the Greek is plural. They all ran in fear to preserve their own lives and abandoned their Master, the one they loved! Yet Peter goes even further than the ten and denies even knowing Jesus, saying crazy things that he never thought he would ever say.

Immediately after this the rooster crows, and Peter remembers Jesus predicted that all of this would occur.

How does Jesus respond to Peter's sin?

Flip in your Bible to Luke 22:61 and read a shocking verse, *"The Lord turned and looked straight at Peter."*

Right in the moment, after the rooster crows and Peter remembers what Jesus said, Jesus Himself, in the house of the high priest, turns at that moment and looks directly at Peter.

The question of the hour for all of us is, what was on Jesus' face?

What do you imagine was Jesus' expression as He looked at Peter?

Take a moment and really answer that question. Be bold and honest and write down your answer. Write down what you really feel. Don't make it nice and pretty. Be gut honest about what you fear might be on Jesus' face and also what you hope might be on Jesus' face. Write down as much as you can. If you are really honest, you will learn something absolutely critical here. (Use the Notes column for extra space.)

---

Why is this critical to do before you read further? You really need to understand your image of God. How do you really see Jesus? How do you really feel about Him? How do you think He feels about you in your good times and in your bad times? What you imagine on His face tells how you perceive Him. To go somewhere new in your image of God, you really have to know where you are right now. Have you done it?

So, what was on Jesus' face? Years ago, when my image of God was laced with accusation and rejection, I would have written down that Jesus had a look of, "I told you so, Peter, you idiot!" Or I would have written something about either anger, disappointment, or disgust. Something like, "Peter, you failed again! Are you ever going to get it right?" or "Peter, I am so disappointed! I had such high hopes for you and you failed me yet again!" Some people might see Jesus as saying, "Peter, you are not fit to be the leader of my church."

NOTES

If you saw intense disappointment on Jesus' face, dig in and figure out what that is about. Where did that come from? Ask the Holy Spirit to heal your image of God. If you saw condemnation or an angry, "I told you so," search and figure out why your image of God is influenced by that. Seek insight and healing from the Holy Spirit to strengthen your image of God to be whole and accurate.

Another good passage to wrestle through relative to understanding how you see God is Genesis 3:9. Adam and Eve have taken the fruit from the Tree of the Knowledge of Good and Evil at the leading of Satan. They are plunged into guilt, shame, and despair. They start covering themselves. God is walking in the Garden. And then God says in verse 9, *"But the LORD God called to the man, 'Where are you?'"*

How do you imagine the volume on God's question? Is it loud, medium, or soft? What is the tone of His voice? What is the color of His voice? Write down your raw thoughts on the lines and in the Notes column. Be real.

---

In my previous, more fearful, tormented image of God, I imagined God yelling at them because that is often what I experienced when I did something wrong as a child. And this was failure even greater than that of Peter's denial! And I also imagined God as incredibly disappointed and thought of the guilt they must have felt because they ruined the Garden of Eden and brought sin into the world.

However, since God is God, He knew what would happen in Eden, exactly like He knew what would happen with Peter. It didn't catch God by surprise. There was no unexpected burst of anger from God because He couldn't control Himself! Hardly! In fact Revelation 13:8 in the King James version says this, *"the lamb, slain from the foundation of the world."* The Father, the Son, and the Holy Spirit knew what Adam and Eve would do even before they made humans in Eden! And they all partnered together so that Jesus would come down and die on a cross to rescue us! They planned Jesus' coming completely in advance of the fall in the Garden of Eden. It makes me think of Proverbs 8:22-36 that pictures Jesus, as wisdom, working beside the Father as they create mankind and rejoice in all of us (vv. 30-31).

Therefore, the tone of God's voice must have been identical to the look on Jesus' face.

So, let's look back at Jesus! The more you know Jesus' character, the more you know that none of those pictures of Jesus as being angry, condemning, disappointed, or rejecting are correct. Jesus would have something on His face that was similar to what He said in Luke 22:31-35: "Peter, I knew you were going to deny Me, but remember that I said I've prayed for you, Peter! Your faith isn't going to fail! I am for you! I have prayed for you!" (my paraphrase).

He deeply loves Peter and the other disciples by telling them that He has undergirded their sin and failure by His prayers! Jesus has done something - He has intervened with the Father and prayed for them that their faith would not completely fail.

Then Jesus goes even further with His support and provision for them all. He prophesies to them to encourage them. He tells them that they will turn back to Him and fight through the guilt and the brutal grief over denying Him. He deposits encouragement into Peter's mind, before he has even fallen, that Peter will recover and that he will also have the strength to encourage his brothers. We focus on the negative prophecy that Peter will deny Jesus, but what about the positive prophecy that Peter will return to Jesus? Jesus plugs in hope and encouragement deep inside Peter's memory before the actual catastrophic failure to give him something to hold onto when shame will attempt to destroy his life! Isn't Jesus amazing?

Additionally, Jesus also tells Peter to strengthen his brothers (and sisters). Jesus is telling Peter that there is still a call on his life and that he is not disqualified by his failure or sin! Jesus is personally committed to Peter, and He still wants Peter to partner with Him in the work of the kingdom and people's lives!

Let's consider a fourth way that Jesus has built in hope to battle the impending shame in Peter's life. Matthew 26:75 says that after Peter denied knowing Jesus, *"he went outside and wept bitterly."* When Peter hangs his head and breaks down weeping in the darkest agony, what does he see? Take a moment and really think about what he would see. Imagine the moment. Imagine him looking straight down? What does he physically see? What does he remember?

---

Peter sees his feet that Jesus washed only hours ago!

Jesus had plugged in more hope against the awful despair that was choking the life out of Peter, *"'Those who have had a bath need only to wash their feet, their whole body is clean. And you are clean'"* (John 13:10). Jesus was telling Peter, ahead of the sin and failure that "he was clean." Jesus knew what was going to happen and was essentially saying, "Peter, you are going to need this. I know what is coming. When you feel like you have failed Me the most, that your entire world is falling apart, I want you to know that you are clean. You are in relationship to Me! You are connected to Me!"

My wife, Kirsty, commented, "Jesus is not offended by our weakness!" My buddy Elijah said, "The look on Jesus' face is something like 'I got your back!'" Another friend said, "I see real compassion on His face because He knew it was coming."

To summarize, there is none of the typical worldly condemnation or rejection on Jesus' face when He looks at Peter. Jesus loves Peter and works relentlessly to build him up, help him overcome his pride, his sin, and strengthen him to care about others (leading the church). Jesus' face doesn't shame Peter but imparts life and strength to Peter. Peter is shocked by himself, by his failure and sin, but Jesus isn't. Jesus knew it all along and loved Peter and the eleven disciples (including Judas) before and after the sin.

Therefore, what we see in Jesus during failure and sin is that He loves us and prays

## NOTES

**Old Testament Link**
Peter's great sin of abandoning Jesus reminds me of David's great sin of having sex with Bathsheba and killing her husband Uriah. Jesus forgives Peter even though he has to deal with the consequences, just as God forgives David, even though he has to deal with the horrific consequences.
2 Samuel 11-12

NOTES

for us before, during, and after our sin and evil choices. Jesus plugs in hope and encouragement before our sin, and this reveals what God does for us! The Devil accuses us of our sin to try to destroy us, but Jesus intercedes for us when we sin and tries to get us to repent and realign with Him. His goal is to get us to admit our sin so that we can come into the light, be forgiven, and then be built up and strengthened in goodness.

## TAKEAWAY

*"No one has ever seen God, but the one and only Son, who is himself God and is in closest relationship with the Father, has made him known"* (John 1:18). Given that Jesus has made the Father known, what did you see in Jesus' actions toward Peter that showed you something about God? Have you ever failed someone in a devastating way? What does Jesus' actions toward Peter mean in your life?

---

It's amazing to see Jesus plugging in hope and strength into Peter before his epic failure to be loyal to Jesus. Jesus' telling Peter that he is clean and He has prayed for Peter, and prophesying that Peter will turn back, reveal that the Father was doing the same things for Peter. The Father helps us and strengthens us against sin and failure!

## FIRST COMMANDMENT PRAYER

Jesus, what can I say? Peter fails You in Your most critical moment, and You don't get angry with him, accuse him, or condemn him. You are the only Perfect One! I love that You pray for him before his sin. I love that You prophesy that he will overcome and get through all of this! You're so amazing Jesus that You washed his feet before all of this happened so Peter could see His feet and remember Your love, forgiveness, and commitment to him! No wonder the angels praise You day and night around the throne of God as being the completely worthy One! (Rev 5:9)

## WORSHIP WITHOUT MUSIC

Focus on these three or four ways that Jesus encouraged Peter before the catastrophe happened. Out of a heart-level, visceral understanding of Peter's denial of Jesus, write two or three statements of awe and adoration for how Jesus responds to Peter's denial:

## NOTES

___

___

Take these statements plus some from a couple of your favorite days from Day 1 to 15 in this study and spend some time worshipping Him. What's your favorite way to do that? If you like to journal, start writing. If you an artist, start creating around those bubbling emotions of joy that He evokes! If you're musical, start creating songs and sounds to Him. Otherwise take a walk, hopefully with a great sunset, and tell Him what you love about Him. But even if it is raining, put words to how awesome He is! However you express it, give yourself to Him in worship and let your capacity to connect with Him grow!

*Have you considered starting a home group or small group for discussing this material? Email Chris@GodIsJustLikeJesus.com for ideas.*

NOTES

JESUS' ULTIMATE RESPONSE TO FAILURE AND SIN ON THE SHORES OF GALILEE

*"Don't be alarmed," he said. "You are looking for Jesus the Nazarene, who was crucified. He has risen! He is not here. See the place where they laid him. But go, tell his disciples and Peter, 'He is going ahead of you into Galilee. There you will see him, just as he told you.'" Mark 16:6-7*

*They got up and returned at once to Jerusalem. There they found the Eleven and those with them, assembled together and saying, "It is true! The Lord has risen and has appeared to Simon." Then the two told what had happened on the way, and how Jesus was recognized by them when he broke the bread. Luke 24:33-35 [The two disciples on the Road to Emmaus]*

*"He was buried, that he was raised on the third day according to the Scriptures, and that he appeared to Cephas [Peter], and then to the Twelve. After that, he appeared to more than five hundred of the brothers and sisters at the same time." 1 Cor 15: 4-6*

*After this, Jesus appeared again to the disciples, this time at the Tiberias Sea (the Sea of Galilee). This is how he did it: Simon Peter, Thomas (nicknamed "Twin"), Nathanael from Cana in Galilee, the brothers Zebedee, and two other disciples were together. Simon Peter announced, "I'm going fishing." The rest of them replied, "We're going with you." They went out and got in the boat. They caught nothing that night. When the sun came up, Jesus was standing on the beach, but they didn't recognize him. Jesus spoke to them: "Good morning! Did you catch anything for breakfast?" They answered, "No." He said, "Throw the net off the right side of the boat and see what happens." They did what he said. All of a sudden there were so many fish in it, they weren't strong enough to pull it in. Then the disciple Jesus loved said to Peter, "It's the Master!" When Simon Peter realized that it was the Master, he threw on some clothes, for he was stripped for work, and dove into the sea. The other disciples came in by boat for they weren't far from land, a hundred yards or so, pulling along the net full of fish. When they got out of the boat, they saw a fire laid, with fish and bread cooking on it. Jesus said, "Bring some of the fish you've just caught." Simon Peter joined them and pulled the net to shore–153 big fish! And even with all those fish, the net didn't rip. Jesus said, "Breakfast is ready." Not one of the disciples dared ask, "Who are you?" They knew it was the Master. Jesus then took the bread and gave it to them. He did the same with the fish. This was now the third time Jesus had shown himself alive to the disciples since being raised from the dead. After breakfast, Jesus said to Simon Peter, "Simon, son of John, do you love me more than these?" "Yes, Master, you know I love you." Jesus said, "Feed my lambs." He then asked a second time, "Simon, son of John, do you love me?" "Yes, Master, you know I love you." Jesus said, "Shepherd my sheep." Then he said it a third time: "Simon, son of John, do you love me?" Peter was upset that he asked for the third time, "Do you love me?" so he answered, "Master, you know everything there is to know. You've got to know that I love you." Jesus said, "Feed my sheep. I'm telling you the very truth now: When you were young you dressed*

Wow, Jesus brought some fish. I love how He eats with them after He comes back from being dead.

NOTES

> *yourself and went wherever you wished, but when you get old you'll have to stretch out your hands while someone else dresses you and takes you where you don't want to go." He said this to hint at the kind of death by which Peter would glorify God. And then he commanded, "Follow me." John 21:1-19 (MSG)*

First, why do you think the angel singles Peter out when telling Mary and the others, *"Go tell the disciples and Peter"* that Jesus is alive? Then focus on the second and third passages. Does anything in them grab your attention? Now, look at the fourth passage, does this fishing event remind of you anything else in Peter's life? What is Jesus doing with Peter? Let's consider the string of failures in Peter's life up to this point. He tries to control Jesus' Messianic mission. He argues numerous times with the others about which of them is the greatest. A little while later, he blatantly asserts he is better than the other eleven and will be the only one faithful to Jesus! And then, in the end, Peter fails greater than all the rest and denies that he even knows Jesus! Given all of that, summarize how Jesus relates to Peter here on this sandy shore of the Sea of Galilee. What does it all mean?

__________________________________________________________

__________________________________________________________

## THOUGHTS

What did you come up with? It is going to be so important that you write down as many of your thoughts as possible to get the most out of this. Scribble all over the lines and all through the Notes column after every question. Why is the angel singling out Peter for the women to announce that Jesus is alive? Think about and feel all of Peter's crushing failures and devastating sin during this last week. It is all culminating in Peter doing what he never thought he was capable of doing, denying the one he loves at the critical moment with oaths and curses. And now Peter has spent a solid two or three days in the absolute depths of guilt, depression, and despair. Jesus is dead, and blackness and misery overwhelm Peter for days. He thought he was better than all the other disciples, but he ended up failing and sinning in a greater way than all the others. The comparison, the pride, and the arrogance would produce tremendous pain and guilt inside Peter. So, when the angel shows up to announce that Jesus is alive, the women are told specifically to tell Peter, because of all that he is going through. It reveals the amazing tenderness of Jesus to instruct the angels to specifically name him!

And then we have this most unusual passage from Luke 24 as the two disciples, Cleopas and another disciple, walk along the road to the village Emmaus. Jesus meets them, but they don't recognize Him until He breaks the bread. As they return to tell the eleven that they have seen Jesus, the eleven say something very strange about Peter. If you didn't see it, re-read that passage above. Did you get it? The other eleven say, "You're right! Jesus is alive! And Jesus has also talked to Peter!" (my paraphrase).

NOTES

Wow, isn't that amazing! It's one super short verse, but it clearly says that Jesus appeared to Peter. In fact 1 Corinthians 15:4-5 confirms this, *"He was buried, that he was raised on the third day according to the Scriptures, and that he appeared to Cephas [Peter], and then to the twelve. After that, he appeared to more than five hundred of the brothers and sisters at the same time."*

Why do you think that Jesus appears to Peter on his own? If you didn't write much about this, use the Notes column and really flesh that out.

After all the devastating consequences that Peter has endured and the resulting two or three days of silence and despair, Jesus shows up, personally connects with Peter, and helps him start to process all of his choices and the resulting emotional fallout. We don't know what Jesus said to Peter, but we know that He probably had a special message just for him and a special meeting was arranged. Jesus knows that Peter would be crushed by his failures to stand by Him and die with Him.

Eight days pass, and He meets with all of them for the second time as a group, and Thomas is with them.

Next, we have the third time where Jesus meets them as a group. Peter and a few other disciples are fishing on Lake Galilee. This chapter of John is critical for understanding the overall heart of Jesus' character. Jesus has gone through the single greatest trial and suffering of His entire human life. He has been tortured and punished for the sins of human beings so they can be forgiven. The disciples have failed and sinned in ways they never expected and thought were impossible! They sincerely want to follow Jesus, but their failure has been beyond anything they could have imagined. Jesus knows they (and we) are sand. He alone is the Rock who never fails!

Let's ask a question right here at the start. Why is Peter going fishing? What do you think?

---

Peter knows that Jesus is alive after being crucified. He now understands the prophetic scriptures from the Old Testament that say the Messiah must suffer, die, and be raised to life. Jesus has met Peter personally and begun processing Peter's failures and denial. It's now time to preach to the nations the forgiveness of sins through the Messiah and the expansion of the kingdom, right? Everything is on track, right?

Not really. That is all true, but Peter is out fishing for fish rather than fishing for men and women. What's going on? Why do you think Peter is out there?

---

It appears that Peter still hasn't had the shame and failure completely broken off him and replaced by complete acceptance and love. Peter is still overwhelmed by the self-discovery of his own sin, pride, self-confidence, and subsequent failure. He

**NOTES**

abandoned Jesus right when Jesus needed him the most. Peter has a hard time shaking off the guilt, condemnation, and shame of his failure to be loyal to Jesus even though Jesus has come back to life with a resurrected body. Have you ever failed or sinned horribly against someone and then have a restoration conversation with them? A lot is put right. However, sometimes it takes some time to deeply receive the forgiveness and turn the corner to sign up for full relationship again. Sometimes it takes time to fully work things through. See what I mean?

The text in John 21:3 tells of Peter saying, *"I am going out to fish."* Peter isn't fishing for recreation. It has been an exhausting week or more. Peter isn't fishing because the disciples are broke and have no money. Why? Remember they had enough money so that Judas could steal out of the money bag completely undetected. Needing money isn't the issue. Peter is giving up. He is quitting the apostolic leadership team. He is thinking that he has failed too much to be the leader of the new church. Shame and guilt are drowning Peter! He is going back to the only thing that he knows how to do in his own strength, and that is being a fisherman.

Let me throw in another reason I think Peter is quitting. Look at John 21:15. *"When they had finished eating, Jesus said to Simon Peter, 'Simon son of John, do you love me more than these?'"* What are the "these"?

________________________________________

You might say that the "these" Jesus is referring to is the other disciples. Ask yourself a question. Do you think at this point, after all his epic failures, Peter could answer that question with, "Yes, Lord, I love You more than all the rest of these guys!" What do you think? Write down some thoughts.

________________________________________

I don't.

I could be wrong, but I'm convinced that Peter is sick of the pride and arrogance that would say, "Yes, Jesus, I love You more than THEY love You!" Peter remembers when he said, "Jesus, even if all the rest of the disciples fall away, you can be sure I will NOT! I'll go to jail and even die for you!" (Matt 26:33 my paraphrase). I think that pride has been ruthlessly burned out of Peter. Peter is no longer puffed up thinking that he is better than the other ten. Peter is no longer convinced that he is the greatest! After his devastating failure and Jesus' words before and after Peter's fall, I think Peter is now on the road to serving others and the new church! He is no longer wanting to lord his authority over the other ten. Finally, Peter is really on the road to greatness.

Well, if the "these" are not the other disciples, what are they? Ideas?

________________________________________

## NOTES

I think the "these" in the text are the fish.

Why? The fish represent Peter's ability to live a life and provide for himself through his own strength. He keeps failing, trying to live the life of an apostle and relying on the anointing of the Spirit. I imagine Peter thinking, "I can't do the apostolic leader thing, but I can fish. I'm a failure at being a disciple!" But Jesus basically calls him out of the failure and shame. I imagine Jesus responding, "Peter, do you love Me enough to risk again? I know you think you fail every time the pressure is on. Do you love Me more than the hurt of pain and failure? Do you love Me more than quitting and going back to the only thing you know how to do without the anointing of My Spirit? I love you, and I have called you. Feed My sheep Peter! Follow Me!"

Jesus radically loves Peter back to life! It is the raw fruit of the Spirit.

Jesus wants Peter to know that He loves Peter and is completely committed to Peter. Jesus keeps pursuing Peter. Why does Jesus ask Peter three times, "Do you love Me?" Jesus wants the shame of Peter's three denials completely broken off! Jesus wants Peter to dig deep and choose his love for Jesus over the shame: *"Lord, You know all things; You know that I love You!"* (John 21:17). And that was absolutely true! Peter is convinced of Jesus' deep love for him and determines to follow Jesus at any cost. That's how Jesus loves Peter and draws him out of this dark pit of despair.

Let's look at something that Jesus did with Peter. It's an event rather than mere words. Did you see it? It is an epically powerful, non-verbal communication He steps Peter through. Did you experience that sensation ripple through your skin when you witnessed something really visceral? Did you notice the prophetic setup with Peter? Has Peter ever experienced a similar situation like this before? Did you have any sense of déjà vu? It is pretty amazing! Write a few notes if you remember anything similar in Peter's life.

---

*Jesus is the Master Communicator! I bet Peter had this wild déjà vu moment. I bet the message of acceptance and calling went in really deep.*

Jesus is the complete Master of Communication. Consider the following passage from roughly three years prior:

> *When he had finished speaking, he said to Simon, "Put out into deep water, and let down the nets for a catch." Simon answered, "Master, we've worked hard all night and haven't caught anything. But because you say so, I will let down the nets." When they had done so, they caught such a large number of fish that their nets began to break. So they signaled their partners in the other boat to come and help them, and they came and filled both boats so full that they began to sink. When Simon Peter saw this, he fell at Jesus' knees and said, "Go away from me, Lord; I am a sinful man!" For he and all his companions were astonished at the catch of fish they had taken, and so were James and John, the sons of Zebedee, Simon's partners. Then Jesus said to Simon, "Don't be afraid; from now on you will fish for people." So they pulled their boats up on shore, left everything and followed him. Luke 5:4-11*

Do you get what is happening? Peter has quit the ministry and is out doing what He knows how to do in his own strength: namely, fishing. They have fished all night and caught nothing. Jesus, in John 21, calls out from the shore asking if they have any fish. They don't recognize Him. Jesus' appearance is somehow hidden in some supernatural way. After they say, "No," Jesus says, *"Throw your net on the right side of the boat and you will find some [fish]."* Instantly they catch a huge haul of fish. As Peter's muscles are straining under the weight of the giant catch of fish. He can see and feel the wetness of the fish tails flapping in the water. It may have started hitting Peter in that very moment, "Wait a minute! I have been here before! This is waaaaay too familiar!" Then John whispers, "It's the Lord!" Peter probably looks up at the figure on the shore, and the hair of his neck probably stands up! Peter throws on his outer garment, dives in the water, and swims desperately to Jesus with new hope! They have a conversation that is private and therefore not recorded in Scripture.

Remember, Jesus is the Master of Nonverbal Communication! He is brilliant beyond any of our modern leaders or communicators. He sets up a prophetic experience through fishing to call Peter back into the ministry that is exactly identical to the way He called Peter the first time! The emotional, mental, and visceral impact on Peter is like a rock falling through his roof! He returns to Jesus and the work of preaching the gospel! Jesus loves Peter by reminding him of how He called him in the first place! Jesus is saying something like, "Peter, the call hasn't changed! I knew all along what would happen, including your pride and denial! I still love you and want you to love others! Feed my sheep, Peter!" How does that make you feel? Skip to the Worship section and write some worship to Him and come back!

There is one more reason I think the "these" are not the disciples but the fish. Jesus called Peter out of fishing for mere fish and called him to fish for men and women. It goes back to the original call, and Jesus is playing off that. "Do you love Me more than these? I didn't call you to fish for fish but to fish for men and women. Follow Me and let's keep going!" (my paraphrase).

Now, let's consider one last critical element. What do the last two verses mean to you? Someone once said to me, "What a bummer to end on. Jesus finishes this whole event telling Peter he is going to die." What do you make of these two verses? Write some thoughts down.

---

How do I even communicate to you how awesome and meaningful these two verses are? Once again let's review some of Peter's life. Peter wanted to control Jesus as the Messiah, and he continually argued about which of them was the greatest in selfish ambition! It all culminated in his passionate declaration that he, Peter, would never fail Jesus but would go to prison with Him and even die with Him, only to crash and burn in a fiery explosion as he denies even knowing Jesus with oaths and curses. Ouch! That's a truckload of pain!

## NOTES

**Old Testament Link**

Jesus' restoration of Peter after his great sin reminds me of God's restoration of David after his great sexual sin with Bathsheba and killing her husband. Later God gives David a son with Bathsheba who was Solomon. Like Jesus loves Peter, God loves David and sends word through the prophet to name Solomon, "Jedidiah," which means, "loved by the Lord."
2 Samuel 12:24-25

NOTES

But get this, Jesus says that is not the final story!

Jesus essentially prophesies to Peter, "Peter, remember I said you are My Rock? Well it's true! Your storyline is going to completely change. You will have a few more struggles and failures among your other successes. However, you are going to stand as My Rock! And you will fulfill every desire that you told Me! You will go to prison for Me, and you will lay down your life and die for Me! You will do it! You will stand faithfully for Me! You will be victorious over all your fears and your pride! I love you, and you love Me. You will witness to all of human history of My patient love that restores any who fail and sin but will turn and respond to Me!"

These two verses are a prophetic statement verified by history that Peter would be totally victorious in all that he said! History confirms that Peter was a martyr and was crucified because of His witness for Jesus. Peter overcomes and prevails just as he desired to do, all because of Jesus' steadfast enduring love for him!

Jesus was Peter's magnificent obsession!

## TAKEAWAY

*"Anyone who has seen me has seen the Father'"* (John 14:9). As we have seen, Jesus is the one and only Person in all of human history that perfectly reveals the Father! What does Jesus' encounter with Peter on the sea and shore, after radical sin and failure, mean for you in your life?

---

Jesus' love, singling out Peter for a special message from the angel and having a special meeting with Peter, reveals the Father's care, concern, and love for Peter after his failures and sin. Jesus' visceral connection and affirmation of Peter with the second catch of fish reveals the Father's depth of connection and affirmation for Peter as well!

This shows us how the Father relates to us when we are filled with failure, guilt, and shame, and He affirms that the relationship is not only intact but that we are still deeply loved. He restores us and gives us courage to keep pressing on in our relationship with Him and our calling!

NOTES

S

### FIRST COMMANDMENT PRAYER

Jesus, I love how You told the angel to single Peter out for the message that You were alive! I love that You met with Peter one on one to connect with him and begin to help him emotionally recover! You were rescuing him from emotionally drowning just like You physically rescued him from drowning in the water.

Jesus, I love how You orchestrate an incredible second catch of fish for Peter to "live through" so he can acutely experience and receive Your love for him! I delight in Your desire for Peter! I'm in awe of You and Your ability to intimately communicate to Peter at such a gut level! You truly are a lover of weak and broken people! You make us truly great in loving You and loving others! Wonderful!

### WORSHIP WITHOUT MUSIC

Imagine all of your successes and failures coming to a head and denying that you even know the one you love: namely, Jesus. And then imagine living through three days of silence when suddenly Jesus appears to you personally! Then He also appears two times with you and the other disciples, but you're still not able to fully shake your feelings of failure and shame? Can you imagine a three-and-a-half-year journey with the God-Man with all it seismic wonders and devastating disappointments culminating in a seashore encounter with Jesus? Can you relate to Peter wanting to quit and just do something he can feel successful at in his own strength? And then Jesus walks you through the exact same experience when He called you the first time.

Unleash your worship to Jesus as Peter strains to pull up the heavy net and realizes what Jesus is saying to him! Create worship statements and write them down as He relates to Peter and the other disciples as they sit and eat around the fire He has made! Then take these worship statements that you create out on a fifteen-to thirty-minute walk, journaling, or creative art; get away and highlight everything that you enjoy about Him and delight in! What captures your soul about the God-Man? This is the time to crack open the floodgates, reviewing your own journey with Him, and declaring your love, fascination, and awe for Him!

Consider a deep-dive online seminar for this material. See our website for information.

# SUMMARY

Why did I write this book? I people watch, just like you do, walking on the street, at Starbucks, and on the bus to work. It makes so much sense to me that Jesus described people then and now as "confused" and "harassed."

> *When he looked out over the crowds, his heart broke. So confused and aimless they were, like sheep with no shepherd. Matt 9:36 (MSG)*

> *When he saw the crowds, he had compassion on them because they were harassed and helpless, like sheep without a shepherd. Matt 9:36*

I long that it would be easier for all people to know God's goodness and be able to respond to His pursuit of them! I'm desperate for them to see evil and the evil one clearly, and run from his lures and traps to Jesus for His protection, love, and the true prosperity He longs to give us. The goal is that we would see who Jesus is and how He feels about us even in our weakest and most sinful moments. As we then know how He loves us, we are free to love Him back (1 John 4:19)! The goal is that we would grow in love and grow in emotional health by knowing Him! And this insight into the image of God would permit us to come close to Jesus and receive both His love and His power in ourselves, our family's lives, our work lives, and in the world as we interact with people.

To draw close to Jesus, people have to see and discover that He is truly good. What I have needed even more than good rules and biblical principles was to know God. I could see Him as I look at how Jesus treated the imperfect disciples. What was really going on was that the Holy Spirit gave me insight or revelation about who God really is. He is the one who is at work.

Therefore, I have created this study so that people may process Jesus' life for themselves and see how good He is through specific events that show how He treats people. Once we see that God is not only good but that He cares for us, that opens up our whole being, mind, heart, and life to engage with Him and experience more of His "abundant life." That has been my overall goal.

So, what were some of the major themes of Volume 1? After thirty years of interacting with Jesus, I realize that one of our greatest needs is to have confidence in Jesus' love and our security with Him so we can, first, be connected to Him, and second, we can grow in goodness. I am convinced this happens when we see His good character! Often people fear God because they are confusing His good character with the Devil's evil character. That is what happened with the one talent man of Matthew 25. He thought God was "hard" and oppressive, demanding a harvest when God would not even give seed to plant. It's a picture of Pharaoh (or the Devil) demanding the Israelites make bricks without even giving them straw. This was where my image of God started when I got saved. But the Holy Spirit was at work! He showed me that God was not hard but generous. He had given the man one talent or roughly $1,000 or 1,000 gold coins. He could easily have bought all the seed he needed!

Once we realize our image of God might be tainted with some of the Devil's character elements, we can start searching for a more whole and healthy image of God. So, Volume 1 is meant to remove unhealthy dysfunctional fear by revealing the goodness of God. This helps us run "to Him" rather than running "from

Him" when we are less than perfect, struggling with failure and sin. How will we ever overcome evil in our own actions, words, or thoughts if we are always running away from the only one who can help us? He makes us stronger internally by His acceptance, love, nurture, and goodness. Our will power alone is not enough to overcome these things. However, we use our will power in alignment with His grace to overcome evil. Often the condemnation, fear of rejection, and shame create a second barrier to prevent us from overcoming the initial sin. We need those dark emotions stripped away so that we can run to God rather than from God to help us overcome the initial sin. Additionally, life is not merely about overcoming sin and evil but primarily about growing in love and raw goodness! That is the big picture and the goal of our lives!

Additionally, we all wrestle not only with our one-off sins, but those pernicious repetitive sins. How does Jesus feel about us and relate to us during our repetitive sins? Seeing Jesus' patient instruction relative to the disciples' repetitive sins with pride and arrogance helps us understand how He relates to us in our repetitive sins. Jesus patiently instructs them when Peter sank, when Peter worries about his sacrifices, when Peter interrupts the holy moment on the mountain top, and when they all fail Him. When we see who God is, it is only a matter of time until we understand how He sees us! This is the seismic shift in our own self-awareness! When we know how He see us in the depth of His care, concern, and delight in us, it is only a matter of time until we start accepting ourselves at a radically deeper level. This deeply affects how we see and treat others. Jesus clearly said, "Love others as you love yourself" (Matt 22:39 my paraphrase). It is both wonderful and glorious!

Throughout this book we saw that there is no one who is perfect! There is not even anyone who will be perfect by the end of their life! So being without sin was not the issue. Responding to Him was the issue. We also encountered Jesus' challenge and especially His correction without rejection when the disciples screw-up and sin. We saw that life is a progression and we grow with Him. That is a different picture than assuming we "arrive" one day and can finally quit attacking ourselves for not being perfect. The former is a good life with Jesus. The latter is a lie. Jesus loves and enjoys us along the journey. His correction and even His discipline are only meant for our good. We are already accepted by Him if we have embraced His forgiveness through the cross!

My vision for the world is that all of us one talent people may have our image of God significantly healed and matured so that we can joyfully receive from Him and use our talent in partnership with a God, whom we now see, deeply cares for us and all mankind.

Some might say, "This is all great, but what about doing what Jesus said?" My desire is that people would be "blessed." That is an ancient word that begs definition. By using it I don't mean, "The American Dream," which in its contemporary expression has a lot to do with material possessions. By blessed I mean that people would be protected and prospered in this life, in their immediate relationships, friendships, and work environments. So much damage occurs in our connection with God and in our relationships simply because we won't do what Jesus tells us to do. If we embraced His commandments (progressively over time) to tell the truth, to be patient, to avoid anger, to pursue purity, self-control, and kindness, many of our self-induced pains would evaporate, and many of our relationships would experience significant healing. In a word, emotional health.

However, to do what Jesus says from the heart (versus mere external show like the Pharisees) requires that we get our motivation "fixed." We cannot do what Jesus says from a warped and fearful desire to "earn" forgiveness, salvation, or Heaven. Those are free gifts given to all who respond to God in Jesus and begin turning to Him. Our motivation then is to do all that He says, not because we are trying to get saved or to stay saved but because we are already saved and going to Heaven! As we connect with Him, we begin to long to become more like Him rather than the Devil who has been oppressing us with anger, lust, jealousy, fear, condemnation, and shame. We begin to delight more and more in Jesus who desires us and has served us and washed our souls in forgiveness by the cross.

Some have asked, "How does Volume 1 fit into the larger context of the God Is Just Like Jesus series?" Volume 1 is meant to remove fears and condemnation that keep us from coming close and connecting deeply with Jesus. We enable this to happen by focusing on His patience, healthy challenge, correction without rejection, and restoration as we fail and sin. How can you have intimate connection with Him if you have unclean fear of Him on various levels? The Bible talks about "fearing the Lord," but this is talking about deep reverent respect of God as the Creator rather than being afraid of God and running away from Him. This reaction is often rooted in the unclean fear He is not 100 percent good, 100 percent of the time because we have elements of the Devil's character intertwined with our image of God. We just don't know it.

If we are running away from the Lord emotionally, especially after sin, we do not yet know who He really is as He revealed Himself through the disciples and especially Peter.

Volume 1 helps us see that God is always good with absolutely no evil in Him at all! There is no evil in God, not even a little bit!

In Volume 2 we will look at Jesus' compassion and clean anger and hold them together as we see that He is both the Lion and the Lamb! This will help us do three things. First, it will help us distinguish between dysfunctional compassion and healthy compassion. Second, it will also help us wrestle with dysfunctional anger and healthy or clean anger. Third, it will help us avoid lopsided views of Jesus. Some churches are prone to seeing Jesus as meek and mild; other churches gravitate toward seeing Jesus as angry or fierce. These are damaging distortions. One of the greatest things we need to see is that Jesus' anger is good and clean and almost always connected to protecting someone who is being oppressed. Protection is a major theme of God's clean anger. Jesus shows us that anger over injustice needs to be channeled through good character to create positive change rather than anger venting sideways and hurting innocent bystanders. Additionally, we need to see how dysfunctional compassion damages people by enabling their sin. Passivity, under the cover of dysfunctional compassion, enables sin to be protected and flourish in those we love. Combining Jesus' healthy compassion and clean anger bring protection, wholeness, and abundant life. You will delight to see Him in action!

I wanted to write Volume 2 for a number of reasons, but one was to correct some potential misunderstandings of Volume 1. I do not want people to read Volume 1 and think that every situation in life can be dealt with by patient instruction, challenge, correction without rejection, and healthy discipline. These were the responses of Jesus to sincere but imperfect disciples who were responding positively to Him. What about different situations in life? What about situations where the people in authority are using their power to manipulate and oppress people in the workplace, in the home, in the political arena, in Hollywood, or at the level of nations? Some of these abuse of power issues can be processed by examining how Jesus responds to the Pharisees. The Pharisees were claiming to be connected to God but clearly not using their power to serve the people as Jesus did but instead manipulated, controlled, and oppressed them. Does Jesus respond to them exactly as He does the disciples? No! Jesus does reason with the Pharisees, and He instructs them. As they continue to refuse to listen to Him and own their sin, He confronts them with greater and greater intensity. His fierceness and clean anger over issues of injustice is revealed. Jesus does not become passive in the face of unrepentant sin.

Jesus, however, also reaches out to the Pharisees time and time again. He eats with them, reasons with them, patiently confronts them, and heals people in front of them to draw them to Himself. Sadly, many of them refuse to listen and acknowledge their own evil, hypocrisy, and abuse of power. They create a regular pattern of hiding their sin instead of embracing His message of forgiveness, and owning their sin to process it and ultimately align themselves with Him. Therefore, Jesus becomes more intense in His responses to the Pharisees over the course of His three-and-a-half-year public ministry. This culminates in Jerusalem during His last week as He intensely confronts and exposes the Pharisees publicly through His parables and dialog with them! Hence, I would not want anyone reading Volume 1 to assume that Jesus deals with abuse of power the same way He does immature yet responsive disciples who are aligning themselves with Him. Issues of social justice, workplace abuse of power, religious abuse of power, Hollywood abuse of power – all are situations in which Jesus appears increasingly as the Lion rather than the Lamb if there is not repentance. So, Volume 2 is meant to address some of these issues and balance out Volume 1. I cover Jesus' different responses to the Pharisees, the disciples, and the crowds in an article toward the end of this book.

In Volume 3 we will look at Jesus' power and humility. Jesus is radically humble, but it is all rooted in His strength and power. He was humble, but He was never a door mat. He was powerful, but He never used His power to "Lord it over others." Jesus never abused others with His power like so many leaders in business, Hollywood, politics, and sports do; instead, He always uses His power to serve, grow, and lift others up into increasing goodness which He calls abundant life! The call is to be great in love, as Jesus loves. Additionally, since Jesus is God and not only the human Messiah, we will look at His existence before He was born as a human baby. His appearance in the Old Testament with Abraham and others gives us an even greater backdrop for His humility and greatly expands our worship and delight of the God-Man!

In Volume 4 and on we will look at Jesus praising imperfect human beings, His general protection, and things like His approachability, self-control, His masculinity, and how He radically respects, honors, and dignifies women!

The entire God Is Just Like Jesus series is meant to answer Jesus' question to the disciples, *"Who do you say I am?"* (Matt 16:15). Peter rightly answers that Jesus is both the Messiah and the Son of God. The series tries to explore the depth of that question in terms of wrestling, not with His divine roles or titles, but with Jesus' character. In other words, "Who is He? How does He feel about me? How do I relate to Him? How do I trust Him? How do I do what He says?" When Jesus prays in John 17:3 to the Father, He says, *"I have revealed your name."* The disciples certainly knew that God's name was Yahweh or the Lord. So, what was He saying? Over the decades I had to wrestle with, "What did Jesus mean by name, since they knew His name?" Time and time again I came to the conclusion that God's name is a description of His character - it is nothing other than His good nature. I saw that the entire Bible contrasted God's good character against the character of the Devil. Jesus' good character in the Bible is contrasted with the character of the Beast (Antichrist). The End of the Age will be a global violent conflict between two houses of worship. People will be fascinated and worship the Beast, or they will be fascinated and worship Jesus. God's name or character is an Ark of protection and prosperity that we can run to and actually get inside. Said another way, we could abide with Him and make choices aligned with His desires. Consider the sketch on the next page. Knowing who Jesus is and feasting on Him are analogous to getting inside the Ark for our journey through this life. That is the larger goal of the entire series.

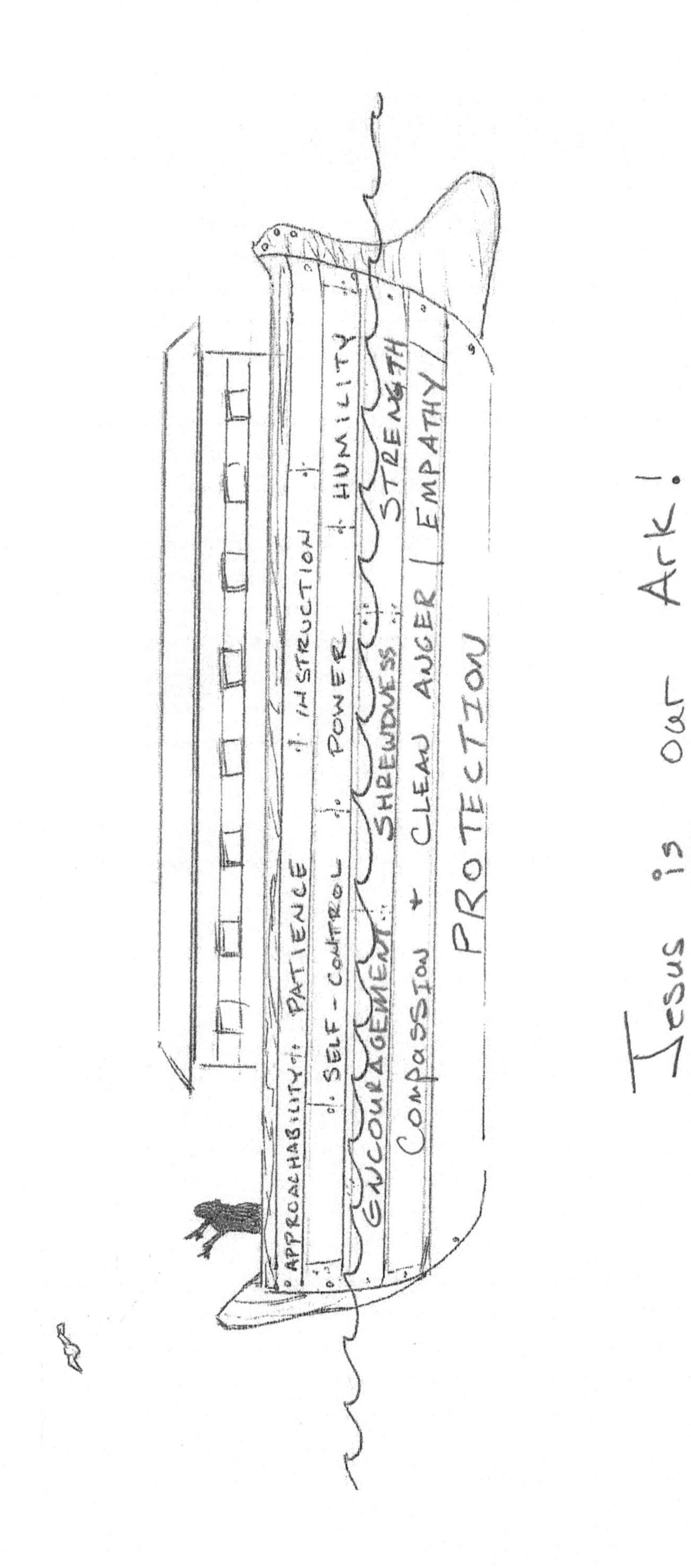

APPROACHABILITY
PATIENCE
INSTRUCTION
SELF-CONTROL
POWER
HUMILITY
ENCOURAGEMENT
SHREWDNESS
STRENGTH
COMPASSION + CLEAN ANGER
EMPATHY
PROTECTION
Jesus is our Ark!

Let me leave you a thought about the future of worship. In the future I believe that music-based worship leaders will arrive who write songs specifically around the subject of Jesus' good character. Currently we have wonderful worship music and lyrics; however, the words are often general. I love songs that celebrate Jesus' goodness, faithfulness, mercy, love, and power. There is absolutely nothing wrong with these songs. I just hunger for more! Does that make sense? For obvious reasons, I desire songwriters that craft musical lyrics around specific events in Jesus' life to reveal exactly why He is so good, so faithful, and so true. I love songs that say Jesus is faithful, but I can see songs that tell why Jesus is faithful in examples. I can see them singing about Jesus' interaction with the woman caught in adultery, or His restoration of Peter, or His fierce resistance of the Pharisees. I can see these songwriters producing a Singing Seminary for people to consume the delightful character of Jesus through music! Oh, what a day! Can you imagine new believers and children learning about the magnificence of Jesus through music rather than sitting in a church, having a one-way spectator-experience as someone talks to them about Jesus?

How can we facilitate some of the change around how people see God? We are creating online meetings for people not to passively listen to a speaker but to read about Jesus from the Gospels themselves and then "discuss" their insights as they interact with the Bible made alive by the Holy Spirit. I believe it is the Bible combined with the Holy Spirit that makes the word "living and active." It is the Holy Spirit that makes the word life-giving instead of a rule book or mere manual for life. In addition to discussion, instead of one-way teaching, we have times to actually respond and do things. Opportunities are created to craft your own worship statements, to process your history and gather times that God provided for you, or to tell your own story that relates to the passage we just discussed about Jesus. I think Christianity needs to be action oriented instead of spectators showing up on a Sunday morning. I don't mean to be critical. I just think we need some sweeping radical changes. In Jesus' day they heard Him speak and then had opportunities to repent, request healing, share resources, or become disciples. It wasn't merely passive listening and then going home week after week. As we have seen, engagement with Jesus is just part of the Christian life. True theology means we do more than mentally consider the concepts of the Scriptures. True theology means we engage with Jesus by the Holy Spirit with our minds, our emotions, our wills, and our entire beings! This is why I have highlighted one avenue to do this through creating specific worship statements directly to Him, rather than only speaking generalities about Him. The latter is wonderful, but the former is available for all who desire Him more deeply!

Make no mistake, we want the best possible doctrine. Paul said, *"Watch your life and doctrine closely"* (1 Tim 4:16). We can never be casual about our theology or else we risk being swallowed up by confusion and darkness. However, we need more than mere mental exercises that do not touch our lives or create on-ramps to encountering Jesus with our whole beings. Jesus said that knowledge was a key to a door, but you must use the key to open the door and go through it (Luke 11:52). Jesus noted that the Pharisees had knowledge but they refused to use it to enter the door and connect with God. Jesus said, *"the tax collectors and the prostitutes are entering the kingdom of God ahead of you [Pharisees]"* (Matt 21:31). Fascinatingly, the tax collectors and prostitutes (and the disciples) were using the key of knowledge to respond to the Holy One of Israel! The issue is not knowledge (The Tree of the Knowledge of Good and Evil), but the real issue with humans and God is life and encountering God through the gospel (The Tree of Life).

I hope you read this book a hundred times. I hope you do more than read it. I hope you mark it up and scribble all over it as you chew on His incredibly wonderful character and nourish yourself on His radically unique goodness! I hope you use it to craft your own worship and fascination statements! I hope you enlarge your space to worship with or without music! I hope you create a place you can go anytime in your car, at work, at home, in between meetings, to connect with God, receive His love and power, and be strengthened to care about people in your life. We want to ask God for things in prayer that we need (petition), and we want to be honest about our failures and sins (confession), but what about worshiping God with a significant part of our prayer time? We can live life and worship Him on the journey, along the way, through the ups and the downs. He is "with" us. He IS our Ark!

Worship, not law, leads to transformation.

He delights in us! Let us respond and delight in Him!

All God's Best!

*Chris Sarris*

# A PRETEND ARGUMENT AMONG THE DISCIPLES

"WHO IS THE GREATEST?"

I wanted to write this imaginary story about the disciples arguing about which of them was the greatest so we can wrestle in a visceral way with the gritty texture of what they might have said. Of course, I am only imagining the conversations, so it is sure to be incorrect. However, it still serves us to consider what they might have said, and it reminds us of the multitude of their success, failures, and sins. Then we can contrast Jesus' responses to them along their entire three-and-a-half-year journey. This entire pretend argument continues to highlight Jesus' goodness to take their raw human nature and make great men and women out of them. Again, perfection is not the issue for them or for us, because no one is perfect. Realignment through the cross (aka repentance) and subsequent growth through Jesus' good response to weak and sinful human nature is the core fiber of the kingdom!

Jesus declares to the disciples on at least three different occasions that He will be betrayed and killed at the hands of the Pharisees and the Romans. After each statement the disciples erupt into arguments about which of them is the greatest, possibly to settle matters of succession relative to who would be the next leader. However, it still reveals their pride and competition which stand in opposition to Jesus' instruction to serve one another. I am going to choose the third argument at the Last Supper as the timeframe to explore their competition because it gives me the latest chronological date to bring most of their sins and failures into the argument. Given this, I cannot use the event in Gethsemane when the three fall asleep at Jesus' critical hours because it would occur after their argument. Additionally, Thomas's failure to believe that Jesus is alive is after the Last Supper, so I cannot use that one. Nor can I use the fact that all eleven failed to stand by Jesus when the Romans captured Him or their failure to believe the women when they told them Jesus was alive. Here are some guesses at what they could possibly have said:

Peter (speaking): Could it really be possible that it will happen as He says? That the Master will be betrayed, captured, and killed by our leaders? Could they really be that jealous of Him? Can't they see that the long-awaited Messiah is Jesus? I can't believe it, but if it were really to happen, I think it only natural that I become our new leader to ensure the movement continues! Remember, when I first met the Master, He called me the Rock!

Others: I don't know Peter. You asked Him about the parable of food going into and out of a man, and He pretty much said you were "dull" or "without understanding." Doesn't sound like robust leadership to us!

Andrew: Heck, I was one of the very first of two disciples to be called by Jesus!

Nathanael: Jesus said I was completely without guile or deceit!

Another: Yeah, but just before that you were trashing His hometown, criticizing Nazareth, saying, "Can anything good come out of Nazareth," like it was the ghetto!

James or John: Well, Jesus called us the "Sons of Thunder"! Power, that is our middle name! One of us should be the new leader!

Another Disciple: I'm not even sure that one of you twelve is the greatest. Remember when Jesus told us the parable of the four soils? None of you got it. You had to ask Jesus what it meant! One of us would be a better leader!

James and John: We saw Jesus completely transformed into His divine appearance! We were there! You nine were nowhere even close!

Peter: Yeah, I was there, too!

James and John: But you screwed up the whole supernatural visitation when Moses and Elijah were talking to Jesus! The glory was breaking out all over the Master until you started running your mouth, and the whole thing was shut down! You're clearly NOT the greatest of us! And when we came down the mountain, the rest of you nine disciples couldn't even cast one demon out of a little boy! Jesus had to take over!

Peter: Well, you guys tried to worm your way to the right and left of Jesus' throne, and Jesus denied you! You even tried to manipulate the Master with your own mom! And He knows it! Remember when the Master asked us all who He really was? You guys said He was one of the old prophets, or Elijah, or John the Baptist come back from the dead. Who got it right? Me! I figured out that He is the Messiah and the very Son of God!

James and John: OK, OK, that's true. But, a little later Jesus predicted His death again, and you took him aside and rebuked Jesus Himself for His master plan! That was real smart! You got called Satan too! Has any of us been called Satan? So, we don't see how you could be the greatest!

Peter: Yeah, but I walked on water!

Others: Sure, but you also sank!

Peter: Well, I didn't see any of you guys getting out of the boat! Besides, neither of you two should lead. You wanted to call down lightning on the little Samaritan village because they rejected Jesus and didn't want Him to stay there! Talk about overreacting with rage! I don't see how the Master could trust you two hot heads to lead the movement!

Another Disciple: Honestly, when the storm came up on the lake, you twelve were crying like babies, terrorized that you were going to drown while the Master was sleeping. Faith? Sounds more like Zero-faith if you ask me!

Another Disciple: Actually, all of you twelve were confused about His parable of the yeast of the Pharisees and Sadducees. I'm mean, you were all frantically arguing about who forgot to get bread for the journey, and He wasn't talking about that at all. You guys all seem pretty clueless to be the leader!

Others: And you, John? You told that one guy who was casting out demons in Jesus' name to stop it! Why did you say that? That guy was walking in the kingdom and doing exactly what Jesus was training us to do! Man, your control issues were really coming to the surface when you were trying to stop him! Jesus told you to knock it off.

Judas: Clearly I'm the most important because Jesus put me in charge of all the money!

Another Disciple: None of you twelve are the greatest because Jesus had to discipline all of you for running off the children and the parents with babies! He was indignant!

Another Disciple: I remember something else. Several of you, at Judas' leading, were criticizing Mary after she anointed His feet with oil. You really blew it that time! The Master rebuked all of you!

Another Disciple: And Peter, weren't you just saying five minutes ago that even if all the rest fell away you never would? Pride man! Your pride reaches to high heaven!

Now, these thoughts are only a guess of what I might say if I were in the "Who Is the Greatest" argument. Jesus had labored, not only by His words but also by His personal example, to show them how to be servants of the people. They were consumed, instead, with being on top, with being the boss! It's in all of us. It's in me. And it's in our pastors and leaders today.

So, the real question this book has been trying to reveal is, "How does Jesus deal with failure and sin in regular everyday people?"

Consider trying to take each event from this book and place it on a graph that represents Jesus' response to the disciples. Imagine a graph where the bottom x-axis is a progression of Jesus' responses from most gentle to most intense. What would you name His responses? What words would you use to describe them? Throughout this book I have used words like encouragement, patient instruction, good challenge, correction without rejection, and wholesome discipline. But what words would you use? Scratch mine out and use yours.

Now, think about how you would describe His response to individual events like the first time the disciples argue about who is the greatest. Where would you put it on the graph? What about when Thomas doubts that Jesus is alive? It seems to span more than one category of Jesus' response. There is certainly instruction involved, but Jesus also challenges Thomas, and there might even be some correction without rejection. What about Jesus' time with the disciples on the shores of Lake Galilee? There is lots of encouragement but also instruction and some intense challenge.

I would encourage you to draw your own graph and work through each response of Jesus and place them on your own graph. Christianity should not be a spectator event but an action oriented lifestyle. Engage with Him and process His responses. By doing this yourself you will grow tremendously, rather than merely seeing my option which of course is not perfect and contains errors.

Once you do your own graph, examine my visual description of Jesus' responses on the following page.

Through the lens of what they might say in their pretend argument above, connect each event with how Jesus responded. Use this as a way to compare and contrast His character and personality to various situations. Let this define how you see Him and how he relates to us. Ask Holy Spirit to grow and mature your image of God.

## THE SPECTRUM OF JESUS' RESPONSE TO FAILURE AND SIN

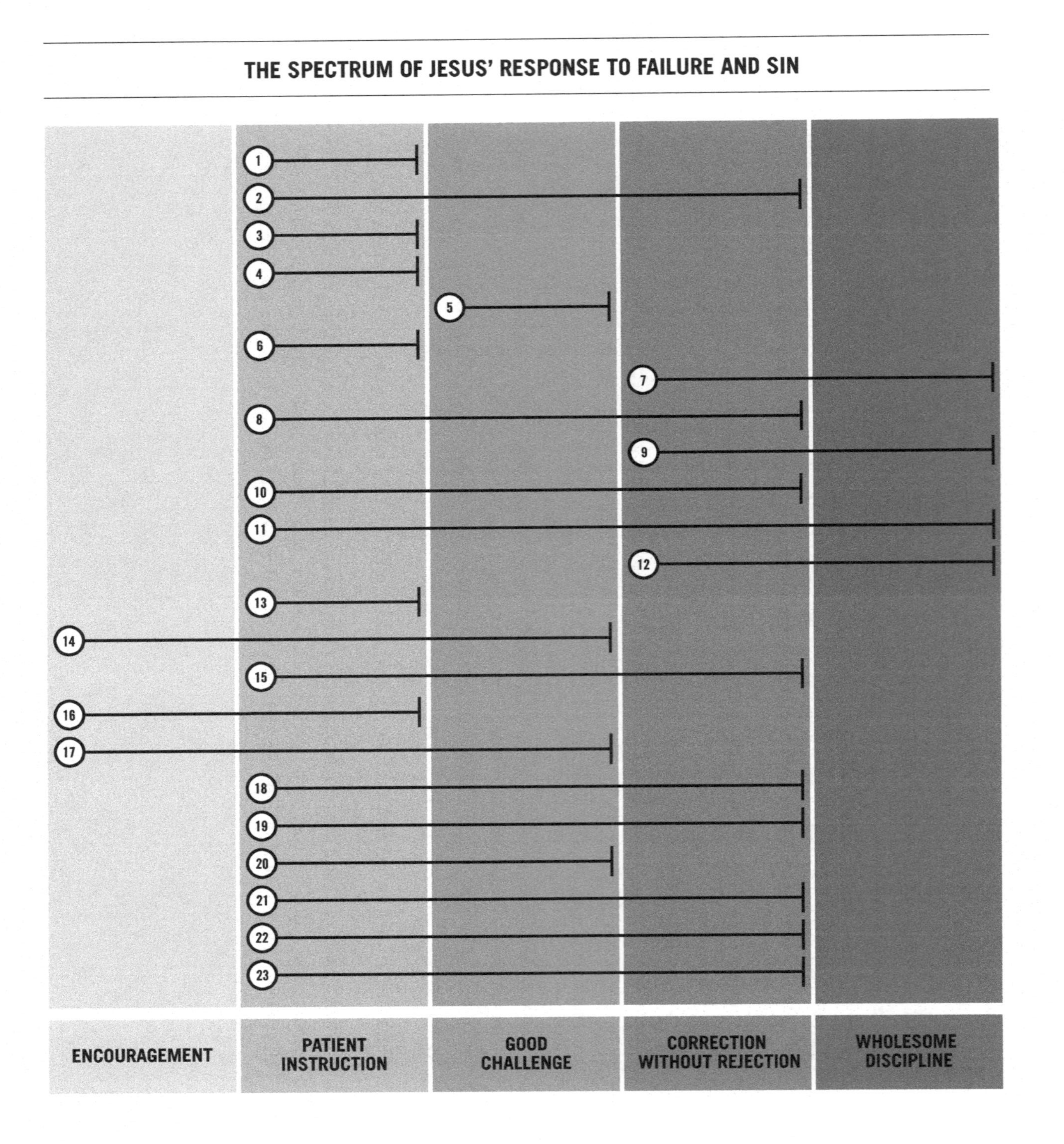


Note

These characteristics are never part of Jesus' response to those who follow Him:

- Fault-finding
- Criticism
- Accusation
- Passive aggression
- Unclean guilt
- Rejection
- Shame

1. Who is the greatest?
2. The disciples harshly criticize Mary.
3. The disciples are confused.
4. Are James and John the greatest?
5. Peter walks on water and then sinks.
6. Peter worries about his sacrifices.
7. The disciples run off the children.
8. Thomas doubts that Jesus is alive.
9. James and John want to wipe out the Samaritan village.
10. Peter draws attention to himself during a holy moment.
11. The disciples are afraid of the furious storm.
12. Peter tries to control Jesus.
13. Who is the greatest at the Last Supper?
14. Is Peter the greatest?
15. They all fall asleep.
16. What was on Jesus' face when Peter denies knowing Him?
17. Jesus' ultimate response to failure and sin on the shores of Galilee.
18. Peter speaks for Jesus regarding the two drachma tax.
19. John criticizes the guy casting out demons.
20. The disciples are confused regarding yeast.
21. The disciples are confused about what makes a person unclean.
22. The disciples fail to believe that Jesus is alive.
23. Peter cuts off the high priest's servant's ear.

# ADDITIONAL STUDY

## PASSAGES & THOUGHTS

*After Jesus and his disciples arrived in Capernaum, the collectors of the two-drachma temple tax came to Peter and asked, "Doesn't your teacher pay the temple tax?" "Yes, he does," he replied. When Peter came into the house, Jesus was the first to speak. "What do you think, Simon?" he asked. "From whom do the kings of the earth collect duty and taxes–from their own children or from others?" "From others," Peter answered. "Then the children are exempt," Jesus said to him. "But so that we may not cause offense, go to the lake and throw out your line. Take the first fish you catch; open its mouth and you will find a four-drachma coin. Take it and give it to them for my tax and yours." Matt 17:24-27*

How is Peter possibly overstepping his position here? Journal about Jesus' response to Peter's actions. How do you feel as you realize He relates to you this way? How does Jesus relate to the temple officials?

### THOUGHTS

The two drachma tax was probably a tax for the upkeep of the temple. The collectors approach Peter asking if Jesus pays this tax. Interestingly, Peter does not consult Jesus but answers for Him. I don't know if Peter was feeling a little pressured by them, but he just offers up, "Yes, He does." Even more interesting is that Jesus is the first to speak when they come into the house. Clearly He is aware of the discussion somehow. Once again it is noteworthy that He doesn't criticize or find fault with Peter about speaking for Him. It's another great example of the patient way Jesus instructs Peter on taxes and, more importantly, on the kingdom. Then Jesus provides the money for the tax miraculously. The miracle itself is instructional as Jesus continues to show Peter His true power and identity.

Another thing that is very encouraging here is that Jesus doesn't want to offend the temple offficials. He isn't a loose cannon like some crazy Hollywood star or political candidate that runs around offending people. Jesus may offend people as He stands for the truth in an evil world, but He doesn't want to offend people, if He doesn't have to. That is hugely encouraging to me.

*Jesus, Your patient instruction reveals the Father's mode of relating to us when we have questions and are confused! I love the fact that You don't want to offend people if You don't have to. I always delight in Your patient instruction for Peter's screw ups as well as mine.*

## WORSHIP WITHOUT MUSIC

Write down a couple of worship statements to Jesus about how He relates to Peter and the temple officials around the temple tax:

________________________________________________

________________________________________________

# PASSAGE 2

## JOHN CRITICIZES THE GUY CASTING OUT DEMONS

*"Teacher," said John, "we saw someone driving out demons in your name and we told him to stop, because he was not one of us." "Do not stop him," Jesus said. "For no one who does a miracle in my name can in the next moment say anything bad about me, for whoever is not against us is for us. Truly I tell you, anyone who gives you a cup of water in my name because you belong to the Messiah will certainly not lose their reward." Mark 9:38-41*

What is John doing here? Any ideas why? Describe the situation and Jesus' response to John. Also, quickly review Mark 9:33-37 just before this event occurs for further context and possible ideas.

___

___

### THOUGHTS

This is a very instructive passage on both human nature and Jesus Himself. What can we learn about the disciples, and what can we learn about Jesus? Strangely, John pipes up with some information about how they saw some guy driving out demons in Jesus' name and helping people! John basically says, "We told him to knock it off because he was not a part of our group!" This is pretty ridiculous when you consider how Jesus is calling everyone to respond and to get involved in the kingdom. Jesus is working with the twelve disciples, but clearly there are a lot of other disciples as well. Remember Mark 4:8 that references other disciples? And of course, Jesus sends out the seventy disciples to thirty-five different villages. So here is a guy obeying Jesus and helping people, and John opposes him and tells him to stop. I don't know about you, but if I were Jesus, I could get pretty upset here. I might even yell at John (but that's just my immature response).

A few verses earlier in Mark 9:14-28, on the mountain top, Jesus was completely unveiled and His true identity and glory were revealed to Peter, James, and John. Afterwards as they join the other nine disciples, they find out that the others could not deliver a boy from a demon. They wait until they are indoors to privately ask Jesus about it. They might have been embarrassed. *"After Jesus had gone indoors, his disciples asked him privately, 'Why couldn't we drive it out?'"* (Mark 9:28). So it is strange, given their failure to drive out a demon, that they find fault with this guy who is obviously having success at driving out demons in Jesus' name. Insecurity on John's part? Pride? Who knows.

Lastly, let's consider the passage right before this in Mark 9:33–37. This is their first recorded argument about who is the greatest as they are coming up to Capernaum. Is there any chance John is feeling a little touchy about this guy's success since he is not "one of them?" Any chance this is an extension of the "who is the greatest" argument in their little circle? Is there any chance he is feeling like, "This is our turf, and you can't edge in on it! Your not on the Org-chart. In the hierarchy I see Jesus at the top, then it's me and then James, then the other ten and then the seventy-two disciples. But you're not part of this!" I don't know. It's just a guess, but there often is competition between Christian ministries. It shouldn't be that way. We should cheer on anyone who is having some success in the purposes of Christ whether they are in our group or not, because this is supposed to be about Jesus and not us. The greatest of us will serve the other Christian, Catholic, and Orthodox ministries and support them for Jesus! Maybe John is struggling with that?

Now, given that stack of events, like I said, I would be tempted to get pretty angry. But what does Jesus do? We don't know Jesus' exact tone, but He basically instructs and challenges them, "Don't hinder people who are trying to follow Me! Get engaged in kingdom work and help people" (my paraphrase). Mark 9:39 adds more instruction saying, *"No one who does a miracle in my name can in the next moment say anything bad about me."* Once again, patient instruction is the trademark of Jesus' response! Isn't he wonderful?

*Jesus, I love Your correction without rejection so that we can mature as deeply and quickly as possible! I love that You reveal how God relates to us!*

## WORSHIP WITHOUT MUSIC

What moves your heart about Jesus here? Keep taking these worship steps to increase your capacity to enjoy Him. Transformation in your own life comes from worship, not law. Write some down.

________________________________________

________________________________________

# PASSAGE 3

## THE DISCIPLES ARE CONFUSED REGARDING YEAST

*The Pharisees and Sadducees came to Jesus and tested him by asking him to show them a sign from heaven. He replied, "When evening comes, you say, 'It will be fair weather, for the sky is red,' and in the morning, 'Today it will be stormy, for the sky is red and overcast.' You know how to interpret the appearance of the sky, but you cannot interpret the signs of the times. A wicked and adulterous generation looks for a sign, but none will be given it except the sign of Jonah." Jesus then left them and went away. When they went across the lake, the disciples forgot to take bread. "Be careful," Jesus said to them. "Be on your guard against the yeast of the Pharisees and Sadducees." They discussed this among themselves and said, "It is because we didn't bring any bread." Aware of their discussion, Jesus asked, "You of little faith, why are you talking among yourselves about having no bread? Do you still not understand? Don't you remember the five loaves for the five thousand, and how many basketfuls you gathered? Or the seven loaves for the four thousand, and how many basketfuls you gathered? How is it you don't understand that I was not talking to you about bread? But be on your guard against the yeast of the Pharisees and Sadducees." Then they understood that he was not telling them to guard against the yeast used in bread, but against the teaching of the Pharisees and Sadducees. Matt 16:1-12*

What is going on with the disciples, and what are they confused about? What aspects of Jesus' character do you see? What does Jesus do?

____________________________________________________________

____________________________________________________________

### THOUGHTS

The Pharisees come to Jesus asking for "a sign from heaven." They aren't interested in another healing or deliverance. They want the ultimate. They want a sign in the skies or on the earth below, something that has no way of being manipulated by man. They want something like the manna that God provided every morning during Moses' time or the parting of the Red Sea. Jesus leaves the Pharisees and warns His disciples, *"Be on your guard against the yeast of the Pharisees and Sadducees."* Now, you have to ask, why does Jesus speak this way? Once you read the whole passage, you realize that He is talking about the teaching of the Sadducees and Pharisees. So why does He use the word *yeast?*

Why doesn't He just say it directly? Well, that's just our culture and our way of doing things, and it's not necessarily better. Remember that Jesus is the Master of Communication. He is after something when He does this. It seems obtuse to us, but it isn't. I think that Jesus is developing ears that hear and eyes that see in His disciples. He is teaching them to listen "deeply" to what He is saying. First, they need to listen for the literal and plain meaning. And Jesus often says things that are completely straightforward like the times that He preaches the Sermon on the Mount. But they also need to listen for a deeper meaning if the literal meaning doesn't explain everything. In this case the word *yeast* begs more interpretation. Yeast is what works through the bread dough and makes air pockets or bubbles, causing the bread to expand and rise before it is baked. Jesus is saying to beware of the stuff inside the Sadducees and Pharisees that motivates their way of thinking: namely, legalism and hypocrisy.

Well, the disciples are as confused as they can be over this. They stop at the literal interpretation and don't go any further. They have no idea what Jesus is talking about. (Peter learns to interpret better by the time of Acts 10 when he visits Cornelius' house and sees a sheet come down from heaven.) The Twelve are talking among themselves saying, "Why is He talking about yeast?" Peter might have turned to James or John and said, "Hey, guys, did I miss a parable? What did Jesus say to the Pharisees? Do you know what He is talking about?" Nathanael or Thomas might have said, "Guys, everyone knows that yeast is used to make bread rise, right? Well, I just realized that we didn't bring any bread. Maybe that's what He is talking about."

Oh, I can just see Jesus smiling! *"You of little faith, why are you talking among yourselves about having no bread?"* How you read this passage (and all the others in the Bible) reveal your picture of God. How you hear Jesus' voice reveals your image of God. What did you write in the blanks after this passage? Does Jesus seem angry? Does He seem amused? Does He sound indifferent and uncaring? Or does He sound worn out, on the verge of giving up? Is He speaking loud or soft? Be honest. (Write it down in the line below – exactly how you feel – whether you think it is right or wrong. The only way to grow is to be honest about where you are and see if it makes sense with the Bible or not.)

____________________________________________________________

____________________________________________________________

My image of God, unknown to myself, was so tainted with rejection that I could not read Jesus' questions without feeling like Jesus was finding fault with them and accusing them. But the Holy Spirit was at work, redesigning and healing my image of God passage after passage, so I could trust Him more and more in life!

The wonderful thing about this passage and so many others is that Jesus is patient and instructs the disciples. You might also read challenge into Jesus' words. He is not getting upset. He isn't getting angry. He isn't fault-finding. He is basically asking them, "Why are you talking about having no bread? Just a little while ago I made 5,000 loaves of bread out of five loaves. I made 5,000 fish out of two fish. Don't you think I could handle making twelve loaves for you guys?" Jesus basically reminds them of the feeding of the 5,000 and the feeding of the 4,000. Then He actually repeats His statement that requires some more interpretation, *"'But be on your guard against the yeast of the Pharisees and Sadducees.' At this point they understood that he was not telling them to guard against the yeast used in bread, but against the teaching of the Pharisees and Sadducees."* He is patient. He repeats Himself. And they eventually get it.

Now, you might be agreeing, but you might also say, "How do we really know this?" As you keep studying the good character of Jesus over the entire four Gospels, you begin to get a cohesive, overall picture of Jesus. All the other passages help interpret this passage. As you know more of all the Scriptures, you get more insight on one passage. What you find out is that Jesus isn't the kind of person who is getting overwhelmed and frustrated, taking it out on the people around Him. That is dysfunctional human behavior. Jesus is wonderfully different. He might get intense with the Pharisees who are the learned teachers of all Israel, but that is because they are resisting and attacking Him rather than responding to Him. Even with the Pharisees He confronts them so they might see the issues in their own hearts clearly. He wants them to turn to Him as the father in the parable of the prodigal son asks the older brother to turn and respond (Luke 15:31-32)! The question of the hour is, "Will the Pharisee and the older brother turn and respond to the Father?" Some do. Jesus leaves the door of repentance wide open to the self-righteous Pharisees!

However, He doesn't do that with the everyday people who are responding to Him and seeking Him. Jesus is wonderfully patient and caring toward anyone who comes to Him! Did you know that there is no passage in the Gospels where someone comes to Jesus asking for healing, deliverance, or help and He turns them away? Anytime someone comes to Him, He helps them!

*Jesus, Your patient instruction and challenge during our confusion clearly shows us how the Father relates to us when we are confused! I love Your lack of fault finding and Your patient ability to repeat Yourself. You are wonderful!*

## WORSHIP WITHOUT MUSIC

What do you like about Jesus or enjoy about Jesus as He relates to the disciples?

____________________________________________________________

____________________________________________________________

# PASSAGE 4

## THE DISCIPLES ARE CONFUSED ABOUT WHAT MAKES A PERSON UNCLEAN

*Then some Pharisees and teachers of the law came to Jesus from Jerusalem and asked, "Why do your disciples break the tradition of the elders? They don't wash their hands before they eat!"...Jesus called the crowd to him and said, "Listen and understand. What goes into someone's mouth does not defile them, but what comes out of their mouth, that is what defiles them." Then the disciples came to him and asked, "Do you know that the Pharisees were offended when they heard this?" He replied, "Every plant that my heavenly Father has not planted will be pulled up by the roots. Leave them; they are blind guides. If the blind lead the blind, both will fall into a pit." Peter said, "Explain the parable to us." "Are you still so dull?" Jesus asked them. "Don't you see that whatever enters the mouth goes into the stomach and then out of the body? But the things that come out of a person's mouth come from the heart, and these defile them. For out of the heart come evil thoughts–murder, adultery, sexual immorality, theft, false testimony, slander. These are what defile a person; but eating with unwashed hands does not defile them." Matt 15:1-20*

So once again the disciples are confused. Is it comforting to see that even the disciples were confused numerous times? What do you see in Jesus' response to them? Describe how He relates to Peter.

____________________________________________________

____________________________________________________

### THOUGHTS

Peter is confused. Be encouraged that we aren't the only ones confused by what Jesus said. So were Jesus' disciples. And it didn't just happen once. It happened time and time again if you look for it in the Gospels. It is part of the process of how we learn and grow. Jesus tells a one-sentence parable that deeply offends the Pharisees. They get angry, but why? They are obsessed, not with the commandments God gives, but with the rules and traditions they and their ancestors have set up. Jesus gives them a quick parable regarding what goes into a person's mouth versus what comes out of it. Peter doesn't understand it! I love this because I often don't get what Jesus is saying! It is wonderful that God writes the Bible in a way that reveals the disciples' confusion! He does this to encourage us when we are confused! God reveals the failures of His leaders in the Bible to encourage us not to quit when we struggle, fail, and sin.

Now, what do we see about Jesus in light of Peter's confusion? I think we see Jesus' patience and instruction as He explains the meaning of the parable to Peter. Jesus repeats the parable, and He works with Peter until he gets the meaning! It is great! And we need to know that the Holy Spirit does exactly the same thing with us as we read the Bible! And He does this because the Holy Spirit "is just like Jesus"!

Next, we have to wrestle with the words, *"Are you still so dull?"* All humans have a "criticism complex." We all feel like someone is criticizing us or accusing us. Part of this feeling exists because we are criticizing and accusing others. Even if we grew up with perfect parents, we can still feel like this at times. In years past the same thing happened to me when I looked at Jesus' response to Peter's request for more information, *"Are you so dull?"* I would think, "Wow, Jesus, can You just back off for a minute? Peter was only asking a question because he was confused! You don't have to call him dull and accuse him of being a complete idiot!" I would feel completely rejected by Jesus' words because I didn't understand Jesus' character. I saw Him as someone who would accuse me, not someone who would be patient with me and instruct me for my own good. It was a complete revelation to me when I began seeing how often Jesus patiently instructs the disciples with no fault-finding, condemnation, or rejection. That shifted my whole image of the Father.

If you grew up in a household like mine where my dad was either angry or depressed, you can really come away with an accusation complex. I thought God was demanding that I do more and more but was never satisfied with what I had done. The brokenness and dysfunction of my past were completely influencing how I saw the parable. This, in turn, influenced how I saw God. I thought God was evil. But I didn't tell Him that because I was afraid of Him. (This is unhealthy fear versus the healthy fear of the Lord.) I was very confused about the good character of God!

It is always good to remember that Jesus didn't reject Peter even when Peter "rebukes" Jesus and attacks Jesus' plan to die on the cross to save everyone (Matt 16:22). Jesus didn't reject Peter even when Peter denied knowing Jesus with "curses and an oath" before a little servant girl (Matt 26:72, 74)! Since Jesus does not reject Peter over these massive failures, we know that He isn't rejecting Peter over lesser failures, like this one where Peter is confused about the parable.

It is also important to remember that Matthew 15 is roughly two-thirds of the way through Jesus' ministry. Peter has seen and heard a tremendous amount by this time. Jesus has been teaching him to listen to the Spirit for a couple years by now. When Jesus asks, *"Are you still so dull?"* I think He is like the track coach talking to a runner who has been training pretty intensely. The coach says, "I want you to run the six-mile race." The runner responds, "I can't do that." The coach immediately says, "What are you talking about? This is what you have been training for!" There is acknowledgment of the runner's training and a challenge to use it. Peter has been training. Jesus is saying, "Let's go, soldier. You were trained for this!"

The ESV Bible translates this as, *"Are you still without understanding."* Which is a softer variation on Jesus' words. However, the Message Bible renders it, *"Are you being willfully stupid?"*

When you start to distinguish Jesus' correction from rejection you can really take his "input" and grow in righteousness and leadership! Instead of being depressed and discouraged about "Are you so dull?" you can be encouraged saying, "I can take the challenge! He has accepted me. He is trying to help me grow! I have a significant role as a child, a teenager, a student, a mom or dad raising kids, a career person, a volunteer in the church, a pastor, or a missionary!" Understanding Jesus' challenge rather than fearing rejection enables us to grow in goodness rather than give up under misperceived criticism. Security with Jesus is the great foundation for growing as a son or daughter of God!

In this book we have looked at three places the disciples were confused. We looked at their questions around the parable of the four soils in Day 3, the meaning of the word *yeast,* in Additional Passage 3, and what makes a person unclean, today, in Additional Passage 4.

*Jesus, I love how You work with the disciples' confusion time and time again because I know You will help me as well! You really reveal the goodness of Your Father to weak humans beings!*

## WORSHIP WITHOUT MUSIC

We are all confused at times about life, about what to do, and about what Jesus said. Write a couple of worship statements to Jesus about His patience and willingness to instruct the disciples when they are confused and have questions.

____________________________________________________________

____________________________________________________________

*Now the betrayer had arranged a signal with them: "The one I kiss is the man; arrest him." Going at once to Jesus, Judas said, "Greetings, Rabbi!" and kissed him. Jesus replied, "Do what you came for, friend." Then the men stepped forward, seized Jesus and arrested him. With that, one of Jesus' companions reached for his sword, drew it out and struck the servant of the high priest, cutting off his ear. "Put your sword back in its place," Jesus said to him, "for all who draw the sword will die by the sword. Do you think I cannot call on my Father, and he will at once put at my disposal more than twelve legions of angels? But how then would the Scriptures be fulfilled that say it must happen in this way?" Matt 26:48-54*

*Then Simon Peter, who had a sword, drew it and struck the high priest's servant, cutting off his right ear. (The servant's name was Malchus.) Jesus commanded Peter, "Put your sword away! Shall I not drink the cup the Father has given me?" John 18:10-11*

*But Jesus answered, "No more of this!" And he touched the man's ear and healed him. Luke 22:51*

What is Peter doing? What is motivating Peter here? Describe Peter's expectation of Jesus' life and mission. Contrast Jesus' mission of heart-level spiritual renewal versus military ruler to deliver the Jewish people from the Roman occupation and oppression. How does Jesus respond to Peter and to the crowd?

______________________________________________________________________

______________________________________________________________________

THOUGHTS

Fascinatingly, Peter has not fully processed the time in Caesarea Philippi when he takes Jesus aside and begins to rebuke Him, face to face, forbidding Jesus to die for the sins of human beings on the cross. Jesus sharply disciplines Peter in that moment (without rejection) so that he will get onboard with Jesus' full mission. However, Peter is still holding onto this picture of Jesus taking over the Roman government. He explodes in an act of violence that Jesus has never operated in, or requested, and hacks off a servant's ear. Jesus is surrounded by tremendous pressure on all sides. However, once again, Jesus is in wonderful mastery of the situation. He yields to the predicted betrayal and yet has the emotional presence to rebuke Peter for using violence to accomplish God's will. Then He once again instructs Peter that He has unlimited power at His disposal. Legions of angels are at His beck and call. There is no need for Peter to take matters into his own hands. And then, what does Jesus do? He demonstrates the difference between Him and all other historical leaders who have resorted to violence to establish a kingdom. Jesus heals the man's ear.

Jesus responds to Peter by commanding him to put away his sword. It's correction without rejection once again. But, as usual, Jesus also employs rational instruction and reminds Peter that His surrender was the plan all along! *"Shall I not drink the cup the Father has given me?"* And that's it. No shame, no rejection, no condemnation. Then Jesus heals the man's ear. Jesus' emotions and character are so clean and healthy.

We live in a world with many supposed "gods" and philosophies. Polytheism is our world culture. It is worthy to note that Mohammad established the Muslim kingdom by the sword, that is, by war. Many other political and religious leaders have sought to do the same. However, Jesus is so very different. Jesus established Heaven's kingdom on an entirely different basis.

We would all do well to understand this difference.

*Jesus, I love the fact that You established Your kingdom based on strong goodness but not on violence or war! Psalms 45:7 says, "You love righteousness and hate wickedness...." You love what is good, and You hate what is evil, but You never authorized the use of the Devil's means to accomplish Your will. In this You reveal the Father's heart once again!*

### WORSHIP WITHOUT MUSIC

Have you ever done something where you totally blew it? Can you relate to Peter? Write down a couple of statements to Jesus and declare how great He is as He corrects Peter without rejection.

____________________________________________

____________________________________________

# PASSAGE 6

## THE DISCIPLES FAIL TO BELIEVE THAT JESUS IS ALIVE

*When they came together in Galilee, he said to them, "The Son of Man is going to be delivered into the hands of men. They will kill him, and on the third day he will be raised to life." And the disciples were filled with grief. Matt 17:22-23*

*When they came back from the tomb, they told all these things to the Eleven and to all the others. It was Mary Magdalene, Joanna, Mary the mother of James, and the others with them who told this to the apostles. But they did not believe the women, because their words seemed to them like nonsense. Peter, however, got up and ran to the tomb. Bending over, he saw the strips of linen lying by themselves, and he went away, wondering to himself what had happened. Luke 24:9-12*

*When Jesus rose early on the first day of the week, he appeared first to Mary Magdalene, out of whom he had driven seven demons. She went and told those who had been with him and who were mourning and weeping. When they heard that Jesus was alive and that she had seen him, they did not believe it. Mark 16:9*

*Afterward Jesus appeared in a different form to two of them while they were walking in the country. These returned and reported it to the rest; but they did not believe them either. Later Jesus appeared to the Eleven as they were eating; he rebuked them for their lack of faith and their stubborn refusal to believe those who had seen him after he had risen. Mark 16:12-14*

*Now that same day two of them were going to a village called Emmaus, about seven miles from Jerusalem. They were talking with each other about everything that had happened. As they talked and discussed these things with each other, Jesus himself came up and walked along with them; but they were kept from recognizing him. He asked them, "What are you discussing together as you walk along?" They stood still, their faces downcast. One of them, named Cleopas, asked him, "Are you the only one visiting Jerusalem who does not know the things that have happened there in these days?" "What things?" he asked. "About Jesus of Nazareth," they replied. "He was a prophet, powerful in word and deed before God and all the people. The chief priests and our rulers handed him over to be sentenced to death, and they crucified him; but we had hoped that he was the one who was going to redeem Israel. And what is more, it is the third day since all this took place. In addition, some of our women amazed us. They went to the tomb early this morning but didn't find his body. They came and told us that they had seen a vision of angels, who said he was alive. Then some of our companions went to the tomb and found it just as the women had said, but they did not see Jesus." He said to them, "How foolish you are, and how slow to believe all that the prophets have spoken! Did not the Messiah have to suffer these things and then enter his glory?" And beginning with Moses and all the Prophets, he explained to them what was said in all the Scriptures concerning himself. As they approached the village to which they were going, Jesus continued on as if he were going farther. But they urged him strongly, "Stay with us, for it is nearly evening; the day is almost over." So he went in to stay with them. When he was at the table with them, he took bread, gave thanks, broke it and began to give it to them. Then their eyes were opened and they recognized him, and he disappeared from their sight. They asked each other, "Were not our hearts burning within us while he talked with us on the road and opened the Scriptures to us?" They got up and returned at once to Jerusalem. There they found the Eleven and those with them, assembled together and saying, "It is true! The Lord has risen and has appeared to Simon." Then the two told what had happened on the way, and how Jesus was recognized by them when he broke the bread. Luke 24:13-35*

Consider the depth of hope the disciples put in Jesus that He was the Messiah, the physical military leader, like David, who would deliver their people from Roman oppression. Journal about their grief, loss, and devastation as Jesus was murdered on trumped up charges. However, also note the times that Jesus had predicted that this would occur. Given all of this, what is Jesus' response to the disciples regarding their failure to believe the women that He was alive?

______________________________________________________________________

______________________________________________________________________

## THOUGHTS

Once again, I appreciate another sin of the disciples! Presently I am up to 31 failures and sins of the disciples, and I find more all the time. They are not put forth by Scripture as "the perfect ones." Their failures reveal that moral perfection is never the requirement for salvation, nor is it the requirement to be an incredible follower of Jesus. Great disciples are not born through perfect obedience but hearts that are responsive to Jesus and realign with Him over and over.

However, what is more important than their sin is the way Jesus reacts to failure and sin. As the first couple of passages show, Jesus clearly communicates that this movement will not turn out as they expect with a military overthrow of Rome. The disciples have clearly identified Jesus as the Messiah and fully expect the physical military victories as seen in David's life. They don't understand that Jesus will reserve that for His second coming. We found earlier in the book that Peter actually takes Jesus aside and rebukes Him for declaring His own death. This shows how deep the disciples' expectations of Jesus were. They are not listening clearly and are projecting out along their own imaginary timeline, thinking they are in the driver's seat. Regardless, Jesus allows Himself to die to pay for human sin and satisfy all divine justice. After Jesus' resurrection the women tell the eleven disciples that they have seen Jesus alive but they don't believe it. What is Jesus' response to this lack of belief? As we have seen all through this study Jesus never accuses, shames nor rejects them. However, He is pretty intense. Mark says He "rebukes" or disciplines the eleven for their lack of faith and stubborn refusal to believe those who had seen Him. Luke says that Jesus corrects the two disciples on the Road to Emmaus, lamenting their foolishness and their slowness to believe what the scriptures have said. This is a classic case of Jesus' correction without rejection! He doesn't pull any punches or dumb it down; instead, He upbraids them for their unbelief and stubbornness! But the goal is to make them greater men and women of faith, not to tear them down or throw them out. This is clearly His goal as He then launches into teaching, showing them from the Old Testament what was prophesied about Himself. Once again patient instruction is the rule of His response? Wouldn't you like to have heard Jesus preaching on Himself as the Messiah? Wow!

And what is more, He goes and eats with them and fellowships with them! He hasn't rejected them for their sin! Yes training and realignment (repentance) are needed. But He wants to be with them! And He wants to be with us before, during, and after our sin. We can never wait until we are perfect to be with Jesus. That time will never come. Let us be with Him now, and let us yield to both His praise and His instruction, and also correction of us for our good growth!

As a final note, I was always crushed when Jesus disappeared while breaking the bread with the two disciples on the Road to Emmaus. I longed for Him to remain with them "unveiled." I desired Him to walk back with them along the road to find the other eleven disciples. But, the Master does as He knows is best in our lives. Some years later I read this passage and realized He did reappear to Cleopas and the other disciple once they had rejoined the eleven in the upper room. And that also shows me the goodness of Jesus to those two! That somehow really meant a lot to me!

*Jesus, I'm grateful for Your correction without rejection. Even here Your stern rebuke is for the disciples' good and for our good to grow up. Thank You for not being passive toward us and for not overwhelming us. I love both Your tenderness and Your sternness with us because I know it's for our good. You are the glorious and wonderful one!*

## WORSHIP WITHOUT MUSIC

We never do anything perfectly, but rest assured, we are loved by Him anyway. Write down two or three statements to Jesus about the fact that He may rebuke or discipline His followers for unbelief, but He loves them anyway!

____________________________________________________________

____________________________________________________________

____________________________________________________________

# JESUS' DIFFERENT RESPONSES

## DISCIPLES, PHARISEES, AND THE PEOPLE

Volume 1 of the God Is Just Like Jesus series is only focused on Jesus' response to those who are responding to Him and seeking to be His disciples. This volume does not cover Jesus' response to the non-responsive wicked Pharisees, nor does it cover His response to the everyday people of Israel. These will be covered in other volumes.

In my growth as a Christian, it was critical for me to distinguish Jesus' responses to three groups of people. I fell into great condemnation from time to time because I could not distinguish between those who were responding to Jesus (Disciples) and those who were actively attacking Him (Pharisees). Like the one talent man of Matthew 25:24, my image of God was so laced with accusation, fear, rejection, and shame, I often took Jesus' intense rebuke of the Pharisees as Him talking to me. I would end up wanting to run away from God instead of running to God because I thought He was constantly accusing me for all my selfishness, failures, and sins. I needed to perform and be good because of this onslaught of accusation and condemnation. Because of this, I could not see the blatantly abusive hypocrisy of the Pharisees as they proclaimed God's Word from the Old Testament and at the same time they were indulging in every manner of evil in their private lives, and they didn't even care! If they cared about their internal sin, it would have been a whole different story. They also would have responded to Jesus.

One day I figured out that sin was not the issue. What I mean is that I saw that everyone had sin in their lives. The disciples had sin and so did the self-righteous Pharisees. There was absolutely no one who was perfect. There wasn't even anyone who became perfect by the end of their lives. That took a ton of pressure off me.

In fact, during this time, I wasn't even aware that the disciples failed at anything nor that they had sin in their lives at all. In some strange way, I thought they were "Bible People" and were therefore perfect.

The difference was a heart-level attitude. The real difference was one so deep that it is hard to use simple words to describe it. The station of a person's life did not matter. The key issue for the everyday person, the prostitute, the tax collector, the fisherman, the sick, the demonized, or the self-righteous Pharisee was simply "responsiveness" to Jesus. This was the main issue of the mis-titled parable of the "prodigal son." The younger brother responded to the father, but the self-righteous older brother (Pharisee) did not respond to the father. The parable ends in an "open" state asking the pointed question, "Will the older brother respond to the father?"

There was merely one group who were honest about their sin and were trying to grow (disciples) and the other group who were actively hiding their sin and refusing to grow (Pharisees). As I have said before, this all turned on their image of God. If people know that God is good and will forgive their failures and sins, they tend to be more honest about the evil they do and therefore overcome it with God's help. However, if people think that God is "hard" like the one talent man thought, they tend to hide their sin and bury it and never overcome it. In fact, we know that buried sin grows in the underground heat and becomes a bubbling mud pot or geyser that sooner or later erupts! And that is what happened with the Pharisees. All of their buried and hidden sin erupted into murderous desires to kill Jesus!

Said another way, it was the difference between what each group chose to delight in or be fascinated by that made all the difference!

Therefore, I didn't see that certain people's responsiveness or other people's resistance to Jesus was the reason Jesus interacted with these two groups so differently. And I didn't see that their internal image of God was what influenced their decisions to be honest about sin and grow or hide their sin and erupt into more sin. What I figured out was that the issue was not sin! Responding to Jesus was the core issue!

In the Old Testament you see the same things. King David was a great ruler of Israel and yet had times of devastating sin in his life. But, clearly, He was a man who deeply worshipped God! A good contrast to David seems to be Saul. Here is another great leader of Israel and a very gifted man but one who, it seems, didn't desire God! Saul, therefore, did not worship God from his heart but only in external religious practices when everyone was watching. Sin wasn't the issue. Both David and Saul had sin in their lives. However, both David and Saul worshipped radically different things, and you can see it from the fruit and outcomes of their lives. They both had struggles, they both had suffering, and they both had victories, but they worshipped different things. The result became evident, not in the tasks or accomplishments of their lives, but in the fruit of their lives. What we worship in our hearts will determine the entire trajectory of our lives for goodness or evil. It's not about being good or about performance; it's about who we worship.

Once I began to understand Jesus' ability to not only tolerate, but enjoy His followers who had failure and sin in their lives, I began to have confidence that Jesus not only tolerated but enjoyed me as imperfect as I was. I began to consider that Jesus might even "like me" while I was in process. I realized that I liked my kids fully knowing that they would screw up and hurt each other or say unkind things. If I could enjoy my kids while they were growing, then God must be able to enjoy me, in my immaturity and weakness, while I was growing. This revelation was the key that enabled me to begin escaping condemnation and entering into a more peaceful and joyful relationship with God! This also led to tremendous growth in goodness!

Additionally, there is Jesus' response to the third major group, the everyday people in the Gospels. Jesus related to them differently than either the disciples or the Pharisees. Jesus' relationship with the general population was to preach to them to create awareness of the kingdom and hopefully produce alignment (i.e., repentance) with His Father. They were not yet responding to Jesus and becoming disciples, but neither were they rebelling against Jesus like the Pharisees were. They were in process.

Now, to be more precise, I am using the Pharisees to represent several groups, including the non-responding portions of the Pharisees, the Sadducees, the Teachers of the Law, and the Herodians. It is also important to remember that some of the Pharisees and some of these other groups were responding to Jesus like Nicodemus and Joseph of Arimathea. Additionally, Acts 6:7 says that many of the priests became followers of Jesus. So, I don't want to represent any of these groups as a monolithic organization where 100 percent of them were against Jesus. However, for the sake of trying to write as clearly as possible and be brief rather than verbose, I have used the Pharisees to represent the rebellious elements of all these other groups.

Therefore, let me summarize again that the real difference between the disciples and the Pharisees is not being perfect or sinless. The real difference is responsiveness to Jesus. This is a heart issue of what they choose delight in and worship! Do they see God as the one talent man did, or do they see God through the goodness of Jesus?

# EPILOGUE

I want to circle around and complete two aspects of my story with my dad and my image of God. Firstly, I wrote as I did with a single focus on my dad's sins and failures to make a point. However, that's not the whole story. We live in a blame culture that refuses to look at our own sin but calls out other people's sins constantly. This is the essence of the nightly world news. In families, this translates to us blaming our parents for absolutely everything. Therefore, let me repent of that sin here and now. I was trying to give you one perspective of how sinful actions from my dad impacted and warped my image of God. However, I want to acknowledge my own sinful actions in response to my dad. I returned my dad's anger and rage with my own anger, rage, bitterness, and rejection. I gossiped about my dad and blamed him for everything, ignoring my own sinful responses. I indulged, deeply, in the sin of self-pity.

Later in life, God helped me start to see my own issues, failures, and the evil I was doing. In fact it was not only things I was doing, but also things I was thinking and was feeling. I am not saying what my dad did was okay. A lot of it was not right or good. However, Jesus just convinced me that I needed to own my part in the conflict if I was going to get healthy. Does that make sense?

I talked to God and got honest about my own evil, confessing it and asking Him for forgiveness and desiring to change and grow. Then, later, my wife came to me and talked to me about my mindset around my dad. She suggested I write a tribute to him to acknowledge the good things that he had done instead of only the bad things he had done. I needed to commit to be just as honest about the good things he had done. That was a little shocking. But I took up the challenge. I began to acknowledge to myself, my wife, and kids that my dad always fed us, paid the mortgage, and kept a roof over our heads. He ran a restaurant and allowed me to work there to make spare cash from the time I was about twelve years old. This was a great blessing to me. I also found out that my dad was very kind to many people that worked at the restaurant and frequently let people borrow money from him. My dad took us on a few vacations, helped me buy my first car, and paid for my entire first year of college which was very expensive, and this was right during the time he was having financial difficulties. I began to realize that my dad really loved me, but he had some truly painful circumstances in his own life, and he also made some really evil choices. So I came to realize that my own sinful responses to my dad's sin also distorted and warped my view of life and therefore of God. I damaged my own view of God. There is a proverb that says, "A person's own foolishness leads to their ruin and yet his heart blames God" (Prov 19:3 my paraphrase). Why do we blame God for life being hard and so easily turn a blind eye to our own sin? I did this consistently.

So I had to own my own sin in the grace and mercy of God and stop being a victim.

As you will note I have used the Pharisees as the symbol for self-righteous aggression against people and Jesus. I think this is fair due to any number of passages but especially such chapters as John 8 and Matthew 23. However, I want to own my own part. What about me? Do I have self-righteous judgmental attitudes and tendencies? I'm very sorry to say that I do! In fact, raw human nature generally has these tendencies. We all struggle with this. I have to be honest about the "Pharisee" in me. I am not a full-blown Pharisee rejecting Jesus but I do have self-righteous attitudes at times, and I need to be honest about those and turn away from them. So, how do I do this? I recognize who Jesus is, and I realign with Him! I try to partner with the Holy

Spirit's leading and conviction and say, "Jesus, I sin at times in self-righteousness, criticism, accusation, and judgment. Lord, I want to be honest about this because I know You can help me grow, mature, and be more like You. Forgive me and help me!" Tim Keller's book *Prodigal God* was a huge help to confront my own tendencies and mindsets in this area and bring real repentance and growth. I wept through this book for several weeks as Jesus lovingly but firmly convicted me of sin in these areas. I would highly recommend it!

A friend wanted me to highlight that although many Pharisees had critical, self-righteous attitudes, it was not all of them. My friend is correct. Thankfully we have Nicodemus the Pharisee, and Joseph of Arimathea who was a member of the Sanhedrin, as examples of those who responded to Jesus. Acts 6:7 also indicates that a number of priests became believers. This is wonderful!

Lastly, I realized that God had fathered me through the Holy Spirit as I read the Bible. God the Father is active 100 percent of the time, drawing us, teaching us, and putting thoughts into our heads to lead us to Him. He constantly tries to draw us out of dysfunctional blame-oriented thinking and into a healthier mindset. He does this for everyone on the planet. The question is, "Who will respond to Him?" As I responded, imperfectly, over the years, Holy Spirit grew me up, and not only healed my image of God, but also matured my image of God. My picture of God needed maturing and deepening, not just healing. I was stunted in my view of God, and He helped me day by day over the decades, often when I was crying out, "God where are You? Are You doing anything?" And He was. This book and the image of God that we see in Jesus is the result of His work in my life which was sometimes riddled with my successes and sometimes riddled with my failure and sin. But He was working in my life, and He is working in your life as well.

Yield to every good thought He brings your way, and speak and sing your worship, adoration, and awe back to Him!

# ABOUT THE AUTHOR

Chris is married to his wife, Kirsty, and they have two sons, Luke and Isaac. They live close to the Colorado Rocky Mountains. The pursuit of the good character of Jesus started with Chris in 1988 when He recognized that Jesus was real. He spent a decade of his life hanging out with junior high, high school, and college kids and loved those family circles. His hunger to know God's heart took him to Mexico and Nicaragua to work with the poor, to Kosovo to serve local people while the country was rebuilding after the regional war, and England, which is where he met his wife. He has served in all kinds of churches: Vineyard, Evangelical Free, International House of Prayer, Episcopal, Greek Orthodox, Catholic Missions, and unaffiliated, and has found great friends in all of them. His passion is speaking, online discussion groups, and writing about the goodness of God as found in the Person of Christ; his joy in ministering is the same whether it is for two people or two thousand people.

Chris can often be found in Starbucks, drinking Earl Grey tea while working on his laptop and keeping his IT consulting business running. He also loves skydiving at iFly, walking in nature, taking his wife out on a date, and spending one on one time with his boys, getting a burger and fries.

## WEBSITE & BLOG |— GodIsJustLikeJesus.com

Explore our website for resources to help you dig deeper into Jesus' good character and expand your worship of the God-Man, the most unique Person in human history. For the latest information on the book, FAQs, Old Testament Link information, and more, please see "The Book" on our website.

## PODCASTS |— Apple Podcasts, Spotify, Amazon Music

Search for "God Is Just Like Jesus" on these apps. Listen to our audio podcasts to help you digest the goodness of Jesus and refocus on Him daily. Use these individually or for your small groups.

## ONLINE DISCUSSIONS |— GodIsJustLikeJesus.com

Join a leader and a group of people online to read about Jesus responding to the disciples' sin and failure and discuss what you see and what it means to you. Also work on gathering your favorite events of Jesus. Develop your worship interaction with Him and other hands-on exercises.

## VIDEOS |— Search YouTube for "God Is Just Like Jesus"

Want to work through this book on YouTube? Watch Day 1 through 17 with pauses through each day for you to be able to discuss with your small group or journal on your own at key points.

## SOCIAL MEDIA

Instagram: www.Instagram.com/GodIsJustLikeJesus.com
Facebook: www.facebook.com/GodIsJustLikeJesus.com

Made in USA - Kendallville, IN
1210795_9781736154700
12.09.2020 1259